SAP Certified Application Associate - Ariba Procurement

By

N. Jerome & Navpreet K

Copyright Notice

All rights reserved. Do not duplicate or redistribute in any form.

SAP AG is unaffiliated with and does not endorse this Book or its contents. All other trademarks are the sole property of their respective owners.

Contents

Before you Start.. 2

Ariba Procurement Software Knowledge 3

Consulting 45

Integration & Forms 65

Ariba Process Knowledge 87

Best Practices 124

Procurement Knowledge 136

Before you Start..

Before you start here are some Key features of the **SAP Certified Application Associate –**

Ariba Procurement certification test.

The "SAP Certified Application Associate – Ariba Procurement" certification exam verifies that the candidate possesses the basic knowledge in the area of the Ariba Procurement solution.

This certificate proves that the candidate has an overall understanding within the Ariba Procurement application consultant profile and can implement this knowledge practically in projects under guidance of an experienced consultant. It is recommended as an entry-level qualification to allow consultants to get acquainted with the fundamentals of Ariba Procurement.

- ✓ Associate Certifications are targeting profiles with 1 - 3 years of knowledge and experience. The primary source of knowledge and skills is based on the corresponding training material.

- ✓ The exam is Computer based and you have three Hours to answer 80 Questions.

- ✓ The Questions are (mostly) multiple choice type and there is NO penalty for an incorrect answer.

- ✓ Some of the Questions have more than one correct answer. You must get ALL the options correct for you to be awarded points.

- ✓ For questions with a single answer, the answers will have a button next to them. You will be able to select only one button.

- ✓ For questions with multiple answers, the answers will have a 'tick box' next to them. This allows you to select multiple answers.

- ✓ You are not allowed to use any reference materials during the certification test (no access to online documentation or to any SAP system).

- ✓ The Official Pass percentage is 69%. (This can vary slightly for your exam)

- ✓ In this book, unless otherwise stated, there is only one correct answer.

Ariba Procurement Software Knowledge

1. **In Ariba, how many types of contracts exist?**

    Please choose the correct answer.

    a. 2
    b. 3
    c. 4
    d. 5

    Answer: c

    Explanation:

    Contract Characteristics:

    There are four types of contracts (from broad to narrow):
    - Supplier level, which covers all products from a supplier.
    - Catalog level, which covers all products from a catalog.
    - Commodity level, which covers all products identified by specific commodity codes from a supplier.
    - Item level, which covers specific items from a supplier.

    You define a contract either as a release order contract or a no-release order contract. A release order contract has purchase orders (release orders) that release funds associated with the contract. You cannot create purchase orders against a no-release order contract, but you can perform receiving and invoicing against that contract. You create a blanket purchase order (BPO) as an attribute of a contract. BPOs can be on both release order and no-release order type contracts. BPOs are sent to suppliers on Ariba Network, where suppliers can view BPOs and their accumulators.

    A contract hierarchy is a set of related contracts that can share accumulated amounts and pricing discounts. The master agreement is at the top level of the hierarchy. Each contract can have only one parent but can have as many sub agreements as necessary. A parent agreement must be at the same level or broader than a sub agreement.

2. **Contract Compliance is enforced by enabling which of the following?**

    Note: There are 3 correct answers to this question.

    a. Subscription of contract items into the catalog hierarchy
    b. Manual line item matching of requisitions
    c. Contract related invoice approval rules
    d. Receiving against contracts

e. Contract related invoice exception types

Answer: a, d, e

Explanation:

Contract compliance maintains and enforces contractual agreements. It is a set of features and functions incorporated into the Ariba procurement and invoicing solutions. In addition it tracks and saves performance and commitment for future analysis.

The Ariba procurement and invoicing solutions also support other options (sometimes called "passive" contract compliance). For example, you can create requisitions from approved catalogs provided by suppliers based on negotiated pricing agreements or discounts. In this scenario, you do not necessarily have to set up a contract.

Contract compliance is based on a set of individual contracts and configuration settings. It provides strict control over who can maintain a contract who can buy against a contract.

Compliance is enforced by enabling:
- Subscription of contract items into the catalog hierarchy for selection by any user
- Automatic line item matching of requisitions to available contracts
- Contract related requisition approval rules
- Receiving against contracts - receipt of items or milestone tracking
- Contract related invoice exception types

3. **By default, PO numbers for contract releases have which of the following format?**

   Please choose the correct answer.

   a. <ContractID>-<ReleaseNumber>
   b. <ReleaseNumber>-<ContractID>
   c. <ContractID>-<PONumber>
   d. <PONumber>-<ContractID>

   Answer: a

   Explanation:

   Release Order Numbering:

   By default PO numbers for contract releases have the following format:
   <ContractID>-<ReleaseNumber>

   Purchase orders reference the contract they are linked to via the **Contract** field.

   With each purchase order that releases against a contract the contract balance accumulators are **incremented.** Similarly, the accumulators are **decremented** for PO cancellations.

Release Order Numbering

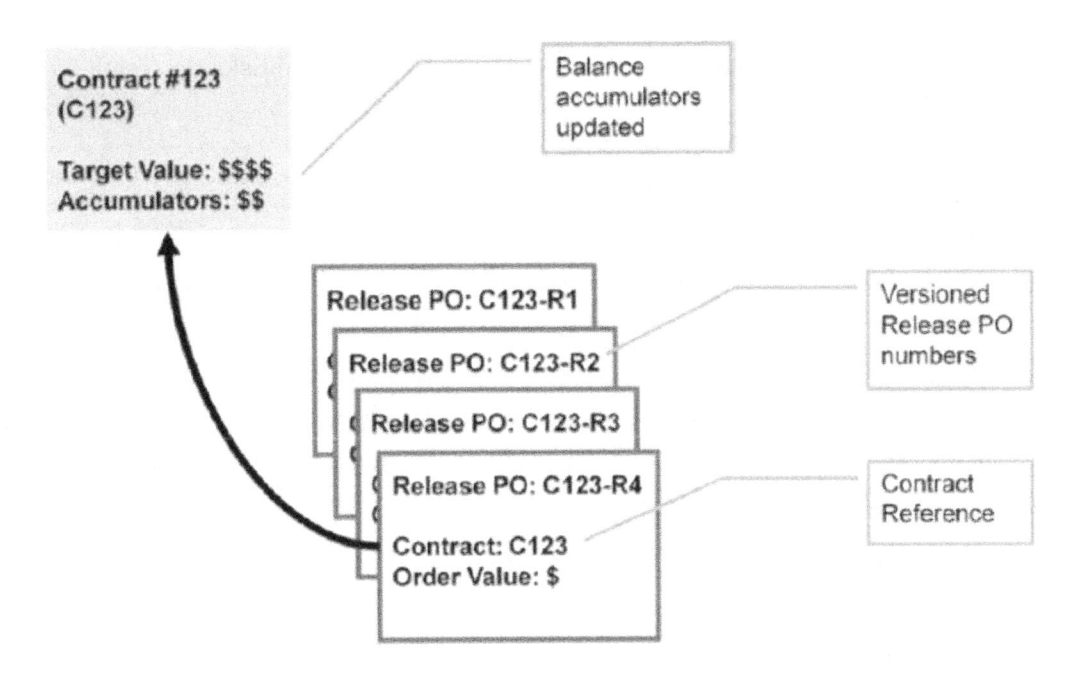

```
Contract #123              Balance
(C123)                     accumulators
                           updated
Target Value: $$$$
Accumulators: $$

Release PO: C123-R1        Versioned
Release PO: C123-R2        Release PO
Release PO: C123-R3        numbers
Release PO: C123-R4
                           Contract
Contract: C123             Reference
Order Value: $
```

4. **Manual Selection Release works only for which of the following users?**

   Please choose the correct answer.

   a. Users with the permission to create a requisition
   b. Users with the permission to directly release (Direct Release Access)
   c. Users who are not excluded from release of contract
   d. Only b and c
   e. All of the above

   Answer: d

   Explanation:

   Release Access:

   Auto-Selection Release works with any users...
   - With the permission to create a requisition
   - Who are not excluded from release of contract

   Manual Selection Release is only for users...
   - With the permission to directly release (Direct Release Access)
   - Who are not excluded from release of contract

-For Auto-Selection:
Any user who can create a requisition can use the auto-selection process to create a release against a contract. The auto selection process automatically attaches a contract to the items that are covered by the contract.

-For Manual Releases:
To directly release against a contract, a user must have permission to create a release directly against a contract.

Note: For both types of release access, the users must not be excluded from releasing against a particular contract.

5. **Which of the following statements are true regarding Auto-Selection Reevaluation?**

    Please choose the correct answer.

    a. Auto-selection cannot be triggered after a contract has been attached to a requisition
    b. Reevaluation will only occur as long as the requisition is not in ordered state
    c. Reevaluation may cause a price change, a contract to be detached, or a new contract to be attached
    d. Only b and c
    e. All of the above

    Answer: d

    Explanation:

    Auto-Selection Reevaluation

    Can be triggered after a contract has been attached to a requisition
    - Requisition must not yet be in Ordered state
    - Item prices may change
    - A different contract may be attached
    - No contract may be attached

    Auto-selection can also be triggered after a contract has been attached to a requisition. This feature is referred to as auto-selection reevaluation.

    Reevaluation will only occur as long as the requisition is not in '**Ordered**' state. Reevaluation may cause a price change, a contract to be detached, or a new contract to be attached. This is necessary because a requisition may take a long enough time to process such that there is a change in the relevant contracts.

Autoselection is reevaluated when...	Considerations...
The contract is changed or closed before the requisition is submitted.	If the new line item price is higher than the original price, a warning is displayed to alert the user to edit the requisition.
The contract is changed or closed after the requisition is submitted.	If the new line item price is higher than the original price, the Edit rules are also re-executed.
The contract is changed or closed after the requisition is approved.	The requisition must not yet be in the Ordering or Ordered status. If the new line item price is higher than the original price, the Edit rules are re-executed.

6. **For Punchout Requisition Item Type, discount may be applied to which of the following contract types?**

   Note: There are 3 correct answers to this question.

   a. Supplier Level
   b. Commodity Level
   c. Item Level – Catalog
   d. Item Level – Non-Catalog
   e. Header Level

   Answer: a, b, d

   Explanation:

   Auto-Selection Release and Discount:

   The system attaches a contract to a requisition line item either via the manual or the auto-selection release methods.

   When the system attaches a contract to a requisition line item, this does not guarantee that a price discount will be applied.

   The system determines whether the discount is applicable based on the type of requisition line item. There are three different possibilities:
   - Catalog Item - the item exists in a local system catalog
   - Punchout Item - the item exists in an external, supplier-managed catalog
   - Non-Catalog Item - the item does not exist in a local catalog

   The table below indicates the rules which determine pricing. Check marks identify the scenarios when the discount is applied.

Discount may or may not be applied based on the these rules:

Contract Type	Requisition Item Type		
	Catalog	Punchout	Non-Catalog
Supplier Level	✓	✓	No*
Commodity Level	✓	✓	No*
Item Level – Catalog	✓	No	No
Item Level – Non-Catalog	✓	✓	✓

*Can be turned on by changing setting on Contract Request Details screen

7. **In which of the following cases can Catalogs be used?**

   Note: There are 2 correct answers to this question.

   a. The number of items is relatively higher
   b. Changes/Updates to items and pricing is frequent
   c. Training business resources with new system is possible
   d. If the contract owner has ownership of the contract pricing terms

   Answer: a, b

   Explanation:

   Release Order Contract or Catalog?

   There is some overlap in the functionality of catalogs with functionality available through release order contracts. The below diagram has some guidelines for when it makes the most sense to use a contract versus a catalog.

Release Order Contract or Catalog?

- Invoice Against Contract with no Purchase Order (PO)
- Blanket Purchase Order with maximum limit of spend
- Aggregated discounts, Tiered Pricing, Term based pricing
- Supplier or Commodity Level discounts are needed
- Spend Limits required for spend against the items
- Notifications required for pricing expirations
- Two dimensional pricing – more than one attribute of the item determines price

Contracts are required for certain use cases which cannot be solved with catalogs, such as these examples.

Otherwise use Contract Compliance when...	Otherwise use Catalogs when...
• The number of items is less than 50 • Changes / Updates to items and pricing is not frequent • If the contract owner has ownership of the contract pricing terms • Contract owner has the skill set/bandwidth to manage/administer the contract pricing terms in the system. • Training business resources with new system is possible	• The number of items is relatively higher • Changes / Updates to items and pricing is frequent • If the contract owner does not have ownership of the contract pricing terms and does not have the skill set/bandwidth to manage/administer the contract pricing terms in the system • If Supplier or Internal resource is the owner of the catalog and its administration/maintenance

8. Accumulators allow the system to determine which of the following?

   Note: There are 3 correct answers to this question.

   a. When to notify users that a contract is approaching its limit
   b. When to reopen a contract based on limits and tolerances
   c. When to apply a cumulative tiered pricing discount to an item
   d. When to reload a catalog subscription to remove a non-catalog item when its tolerance is exceeded
   e. When to keep a contract on hold based on limits and tolerances

   Answer: a, c, d

   Explanation:

   Accumulators Overview
   Contract Accumulators are fields used by Ariba Contract Compliance to track the quantities and amounts that are released and invoiced against contracts.

   Accumulators are automatically updated by certain triggers to provide an accurate balance at all times.

Accumulators allow the system to determine:
- When to notify users that a contract is approaching its limit
- When to close a contract based on limits and tolerances
- When to apply a cumulative tiered pricing discount to an item
- When to reload a catalog subscription to remove a non-catalog item when its tolerance is exceeded

The detailed configuration of accumulators allows an organization to track contract spend at different points in the process based on the business requirements.

Accumulator Examples

Business Action	Accumulator Field	Balance Fields
Submit Requisition	Amount Submitted* QuantitySubmitted	MaxAmount* MinAmount* UsedAmount* AvailableAmount*
Withdraw Requisition		
Approver Edit & Submit Requisition		
Change Submitted Requisition		
Withdraw Change Requisition		
Approver Edit Change Requisition		
Approve Requisition	Amount Approved* QuantityApproved	UsedQuantity AvailableQuantity
Approve Change Requisition		
Order Created	Amount Ordered* QuantityOrdered	MinQuantity MaxQuantity
Receipt Received	Amount Received* QuantityReceived	
Invoice Reconciled	Amount Reconciled* QuantityReconciled	

* At header and item level

9. **Which of the following statements are true regarding Preload Accumulators?**

   Note: There are 3 correct answers to this question.

   a. The preload amount field lets users specify an amount of prior spend against an existing contract
   b. Preload amounts are tracked at the header level only
   c. They are used to update item or commodity level accumulators
   d. They only affect pricing discounts in supplier level contracts
   e. They affect tiered pricing calculation in all types of contracts

   Answer: a, b, d

Explanation:

Preload Accumulators

- Used to indicate prior spend against existing contracts
- Tracked only at the header level
- Affect spend accumulation and tiered pricing only in supplier level contracts

```
Preload Amount

Enter a preload amount to preset the spend accumulators for the contract, for example, to reflect prior spending on this contract

        Preload Amount              USD.
```

The preload amount field lets users specify an amount of prior spend against an existing contract.

Preload amounts are tracked at the header level only, and are not used to update item or commodity level accumulators. For this reason, they only affect pricing discounts and tiered pricing calculation in supplier level contracts.

10. **Which of the following statements are true regarding Accumulator Updates?**

    Please choose the correct answer.

    a. In contracts for which invoicing is enabled, invoicing-related accumulators are updated when invoice reconciliation documents are approved
    b. In contracts for which receiving is enabled, receiving-related accumulators are updated when receipts are processed.
    c. Both a and b
    d. None of the above

    Answer: c

    Explanation:

    Preload Accumulators:

    The preload amount field lets users specify an amount of prior spend against an existing contract.

    Preload amounts are tracked at the header level only, and are not used to update item or commodity level accumulators. For this reason, they only affect pricing discounts and tiered pricing calculation in supplier level contracts.

Accumulator Updates:

- Invoice related accumulators updated when invoice reconciliation is approved
- Receiving related accumulators updated when receipts are processed

In contracts for which invoicing is enabled, invoicing-related accumulators are updated when invoice reconciliation documents are approved.

In contracts for which receiving is enabled, receiving-related accumulators are updated when receipts are processed.

11. **Which of the following statements are true regarding Agreements without Releases?**

    Please choose the correct answer.

    a. No-release Order Contracts do not allow release orders to be issued against them
    b. May allow direct receiving and invoicing
    c. Provide additional pricing terms
    d. Only a and b
    e. All of the above

- No-release Order Contracts do not allow release orders to be issued against them
- May allow direct receiving and invoicing
- Provide additional pricing terms
    - Fixed and Recurring fee items
    - Costs and Expenses
    - Milestones

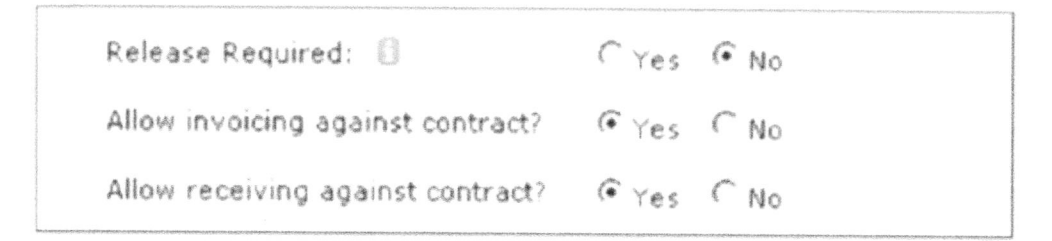

Release Required:	○ Yes	● No
Allow invoicing against contract?	● Yes	○ No
Allow receiving against contract?	● Yes	○ No

Agreements without release orders are a good way to manage categories that do not use the typical purchase order process. This is a common need for services contracts as well as those involving facilities and maintenance.

These types of contracts are usually created to allow direct invoicing and receiving. In addition, they provide access to additional pricing terms for fixed and recurring fee items and costs and expenses.

To create an agreement without release orders, set the **Release Required?** Indicator in the contract request wizard to **No.**

12. **No-release order contracts are typically used for services and need to handle which of the following aspects of service procurement?**

    Note: There are 3 correct answers to this question.

    a. Complexity
    b. Deliverables and milestones
    c. Recurring and fixed costs
    d. Need for more detailed effort analysis
    e. Need for more detailed analysis of resource utilization

    Answer: a, b, c

    Explanation:

    No-release Order Contracts:

    - Non-PO process often used for services
    - More complex than PO-based procurement
    - Deliverables and milestones
        - Payment may be based on their completion
    - Recurring and fixed costs
    - Service costs may not be able to be forecast exactly
    - Monitoring more involved:
        - Quality of work, completion of deliverables
        - Services delivered / charged
        - Ongoing payments

    No-release order contracts are typically used for services and need to handle the following aspects of service procurement:

    - **Complexity** - doesn't fit the standard PO-based procurement process
    - **Deliverables and milestones** - requires a way to track milestone completion for payment
    - **Recurring and fixed costs** - requires direct invoicing, sometimes on a recurring schedule
    - **Difficulty in forecasting costs** - details of what was provided may not be available until work is completed
    - **Need for more detailed monitoring** - requires ways of tracking quality, completion, what was delivered, what was invoiced, and when to release payment

You can use agreements without release orders for service procurement processes that do not use purchase orders. In addition to service contracts, there are other ways you can use non-release order contracts.

13. **Which of the following statement(s) is/are true?**

    Note: There are 2 correct answers to this question.

    a. In the absence of a purchase order, the three-way match becomes Invoice-Contract-Receipt
    b. If receiving is enabled, Ariba will perform a two-way match between the
    Contract and Invoice.
    c. When creating a contract without release orders, users can receive directly against the contract
    d. If receiving is not enabled, Ariba will perform a three-way match between the
    Contract, Receipt, and Invoice

    Answer: a, c

    Explanation:

    Invoicing and Receiving Against the Contract

    Receiving
    When creating a contract without release orders, users can receive directly against the contract. When direct receiving is enabled for a contract, users can receive against items on the contract in much the same way as they receive against items on a purchase order.

    Three Way Match
    The advantage of enabling invoicing and receiving in non-release order contracts is that it enables you to do three-way matching in the invoice reconciliation process. In the absence of a purchase order, the three-way match becomes **Invoice-Contract-Receipt.**

    If receiving is not enabled you can do a two-way match between the invoice and contract.

Receiving and Three-Way Match

- If enabled, users can receive against the contract

- If receiving is enabled, Ariba will perform a three-way match between the Contract, Receipt, and Invoice

- If receiving is not enabled, Ariba will perform a two-way match between the Contract and Invoice. You may wish to consider additional invoice-level approvals for these use cases

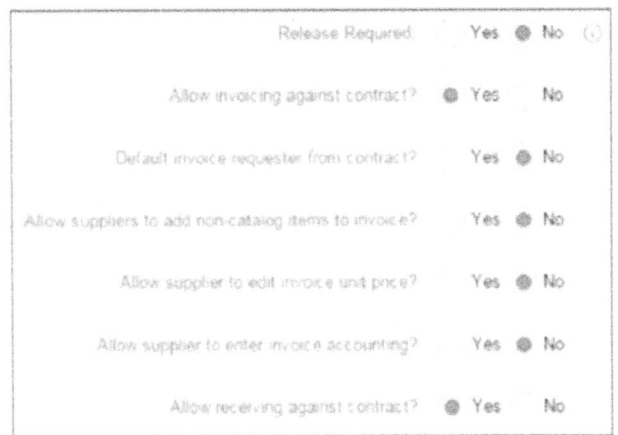

14. **Which of the following are the approvable documents that are used in contract receiving?**

    Please choose the correct answer.

    a. Receipt
    b. Milestone Tracker
    c. Both a and b
    d. None of the above

    Answer: c

    Explanation:

    Receiving Approvables:

    - Receipt for materials and services
        - Users with Direct Release permission (Contract Managers)
    - Milestone tracker for milestones
        - User selected as verifier for milestone

    There are two approvable documents that are used in contract receiving:

Receipt - used to track the receipt of material and service items. This is the same approvable used to track receipts against purchase orders. In order to receive material and service items directly against a contract, a user needs the *DirectReleaseContract* permission (in the default configuration this is granted to *Contract Managers*).

Milestone Tracker - used to track completion of milestones. Users may approve milestones when they are selected as the verifier for that milestone.
Specific approval rules determine the approval flow for these two approvables.

15. **Which of the following contract fields are excluded from change?**

    Note: There are 3 correct answers to this question.

    a. Supplier
    b. Contract Type
    c. Parent Agreement
    d. Hierarchy Node
    e. Invoice

    Answer: a, b, c

    Explanation:

    Fields Excluded from Change:

    Certain contract fields are excluded from change. They are listed below:
    - Supplier
    - Release Required?
    - Related Contract ID
    - Hierarchical Type
    - Contract Type
    - Parent Agreement
    - Currency

16. **Which of the following statements are true regarding Contract Catalog Subscriptions?**

    Please choose the correct answer.

    a. Subscriptions are created using **Auto-Catalog Creation** and are only used in conjunction with the item level contracts that include one or more non-catalog items.
    b. With Auto-Catalog Creation, items are searchable just like with any other catalog.
    c. Email notification is sent when catalog import, activation, or deactivation fails.
    d. Only a and b
    e. All of the above

Answer: e

Explanation:

Contract Catalog Subscriptions:

A non-catalog item is an item that does not already exist in the system catalog. Contract catalog subscriptions are the implementation mechanism used within the system to make non-catalog contract items temporarily available in the catalog.

These subscriptions enable users to search non-catalog contract items as if they were regular catalog items. They are also the vehicle used to manage item visibility in accordance with the contract validity period.

Subscriptions are created using **Auto-Catalog Creation** and are only used in conjunction with the item level contracts that include one or more non-catalog items.

With Auto-Catalog Creation, items are searchable just like with any other catalog.
Email notification is sent when catalog import, activation, or deactivation fails.

Auto-catalog Creation – Additional Processing States:
- Added Processing and Processed states
- Indicate contract subscription import status

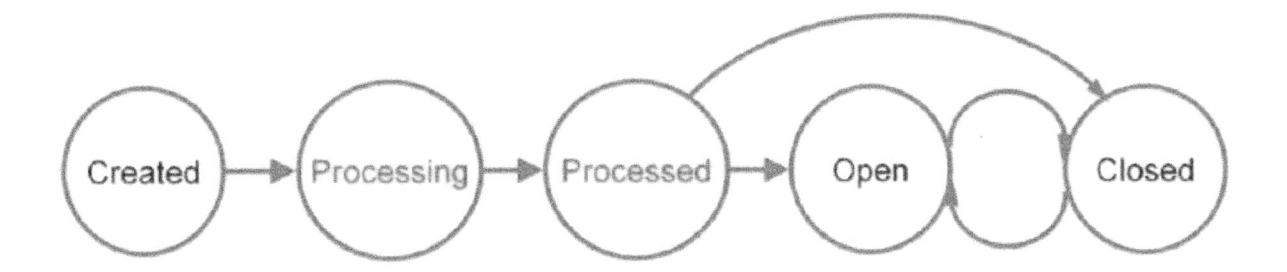

Created → Processing → Processed → Open → Closed

The **Processing** and **Processed** states indicate the import status of a contract subscription.

Unless the effective date is in the future, the '**Processed**' state will rarely be observable, as the contract typically moves into **Open** state very quickly.

17. **Which of the following statements are true regarding Ariba Mobile?**

    Please choose the correct answer.

    a. While you may activate multiple devices for the same user account, you cannot set up one single device to use multiple Ariba users or realms at this time.

b. The Deactivate Mobile Device option will allow you to remove access for a specified mobile device that was previously paired with your user login
c. Both a and b
d. None of the above

Answer: c

Explanation:

Activate Your Device:

You must "pair" your mobile device with an Ariba site using the **Activate Mobile Device** option in the **Preferences** menu. Note that, while you may activate multiple devices for the same user account, you cannot set up one single device to use multiple Ariba users or realms at this time.

The **Deactivate Mobile Device** option will allow you to remove access for a specified mobile device that was previously paired with your user login.

Activate Your Device

- Once you have been assigned to the appropriate groups, an Activate Mobile Device option will appear in your User Preferences menu
- Enter the code generated by the Ariba Mobile app when you run it for the first time
- You can use the Deactivate Mobile Device option later to unpair your device from your user account
- You can pair multiple mobile devices to the same user account

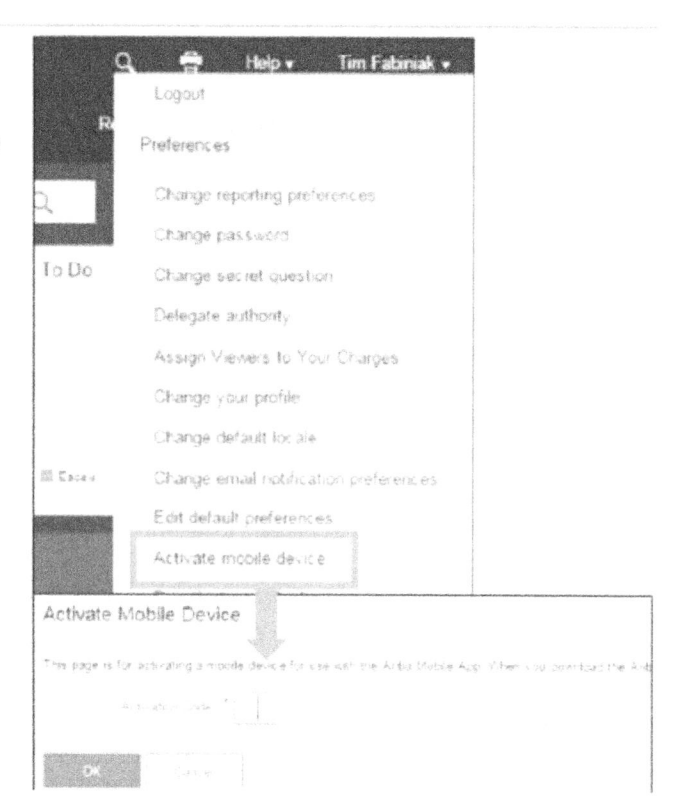

18. **Which of the following statements are true regarding Search Filters?**

    Note: There are 3 correct answers to this question.

a. You can display specific search filters
b. Members of the Report Manager group can save searches for use by everyone
c. Search filters are available in only the Search page, not the Search box.
d. Searching always performs partial matching
e. You cannot hide search filters

Answer: a, b, c

Explanation:

Search Filters:

Use search filters to further refine your search. Filters are available in only the Search page, not the Search box.

By default, searches for some types of documents include a custom date range in the search criteria in order to improve search performance. For example, the default date range for requisitions and purchase orders is 14 days and for expense reports and travel authorizations it is three months. You can change the date range or turn off the Date Created search option.

Searching performs partial matching except for invoices associated with a specific purchase order. For example, if you have two documents titled "Requisition for laptops," and "Requisition for desktops," and you enter "Requisition" in the Title box, both documents are displayed. However, if you search for invoices by filtering on Order ID, the system displays only invoices for purchase orders that match the Order ID search string exactly.

Search Customization and Saving Searches:
- You can display or hide specific search filters
- You can save your frequently used searches. They are available in:
    - The navigation panel of the Search page
    - The Search content item
    - New Dashboard content items
- Members of the Report Manager group can save searches for use by everyone

19. **Which of the following are the major locations for reports?**

    Note: There are 3 correct answers to this question.

    a. Dynamic Workspace
    b. Prepackaged Reports
    c. Public Reports
    d. Personal Workspace
    e. Public Workspace

    Answer: b, c, d

Explanation:

Reporting Features:

There are three major locations for reports: Prepackaged Reports, Public Reports, and Personal Workspace. Prepackaged reports are basic reports created by Ariba that are relatively generic. Public reports are custom reports created by your administrator and can be accessed by anyone with the proper permissions. A Personal Workspace is the virtual folder for all personal reports that you have saved.

Reports give you access to complex business information from multiple sources such as expense reports, purchase requisitions, travel requests, purchase orders, and invoices. They allow you to analyze buying and spending patterns for yourself, your department, or your entire organization.

Reports display data in a pivot table that you can manipulate to see different scenarios for the data. Pivot tables allow you to filter, slice, and drill down into the information to see patterns and relationships, summary information, and detail at the same time. Before you run a report, you select basic filters and set advanced filter and display options to better focus the report results.

20. **In Collaborative Requisitioning, how many types of bidding exist?**

   Please choose the correct answer.

   a. 2
   b. 3
   c. 4
   d. 5

   Answer: b

   Explanation:

   Collaborative Requisitioning: Bidding Transparency
   When you create a collaborative requisition, you set bidding transparency, which determines how much bidding information is available to the supplier. Setting the transparency involves choosing a bidding type, which impacts the available bidding properties. A bidding type encapsulates bidding property fields in a single object. Frequently-used sets of bidding properties can be preset and saved as named objects for re-use.
   There are three kinds of bidding types:
   - **System:** The default configuration at the site level. The system bidding types are:
     - **Closed:** No bidding fields are visible
     - **Open - Amount:** Lowest amount and price
     - **Open - Amount, Rank:** Lowest amount, price, proposal rank, and supplier rank
     - **Open - Amount, Rank, Supplier:** Lowest amount, price, lowest supplier, proposal rank, and supplier rank
   - **New:** Created by a user on a per-collaboration (one-time) basis. A new bidding type cannot be reused in future collaborations.
   - **None:** No bidding information is available.

Approval Phases

Pre-Collaboration Approvals → **Begin Collaboration** → Collaboration → **End Collaboration** → Post-Collaboration Approvals

21. **Which of the following statements are true regarding N Bids and a Buy?**

    Please choose the correct answer.

    a. Require collaboration with a minimum number of suppliers
    b. Used for both goods and services
    c. Both a and b
    d. None of the above

    Answer: c

    Explanation:

    N Bids and a Buy:

    - Require collaboration with a minimum number of suppliers
    - Enforce through N Bids and a Buy policy
        - Set minimum number of suppliers
        - Set fields used in the requisition
        - Set terms and conditions
        - Set violation handling
    - Use for both goods and services

    Some organizations require purchasing agents to collaborate with a minimum number of suppliers and receive their bids before completing the purchasing process.

To enforce this rule, your organization can define an N Bids and a Buy policy where you specify the minimum number of suppliers that need to be invited for collaboration, the fields that the policy is based on, and the terms of the policy. For example, your organization can create a policy specifying that all purchasing agents must collaborate with a minimum of three suppliers if the requisition amount exceeds $1,000 for an item of commodity code 8012. The N Bids and a Buy policy can be enforced when procuring both goods and services items.

Your organization can also specify whether violations of the policy are allowed. For example, you can specify whether purchasing agents can still submit requisitions when they do not invite the minimum number of suppliers or not.

22. **Which of the following statements are true regarding Reporting features?**

    Note: There are 3 correct answers to this question.

    a. Public reports are custom reports created by your Ariba administrator and can be accessed by anyone with the proper permissions.
    b. Reports display data in a pivot table that you can manipulate to see different scenarios for the data
    c. Scheduling reports provides report storage and distribution.
    d. You cannot send the results of a report to your dashboard.
    e. A Public Workspace is the virtual folder for all personal reports that you have saved

    Answer: a, b, c

    Explanation:

    Reporting Features:

    - Prepackaged and Public reports
    - Personal Workspace
    - Reports can display multiple levels of data
    - Display results in the application or export to Excel
    - Display reports on your dashboard
    - You can schedule reports to run at regular intervals

    Prepackaged reports are based on basic reporting functions. Public reports are custom reports created by your Ariba administrator and can be accessed by anyone with the proper permissions. A Personal Workspace is the virtual folder for all personal reports that you have saved.

    Reports give you access to complex business information from multiple sources such as requisitions, purchase orders, and invoices. They allow you to analyze buying and spending patterns for yourself, your department, or your entire organization.

    Reports display data in a pivot table that you can manipulate to see different scenarios for the data. Pivot tables allow you to filter, slice, and drill down into the information to see patterns and relationships, summary information, and detail at the same time. Before you run a report, you select basic filters and set advanced filter and display options to better focus the report results.

You can view reports in Excel format, allowing you to sort, format, and perform other Excel operations on the data. You can also send the results of a report to your dashboard. You can schedule reports to run at regular intervals. Scheduling reports provides report storage and distribution.

23. **Which of the following are the advantages of Ariba e-Archive?**

    Note: There are 3 correct answers to this question.

    a. Easy access to Excel view of invoices
    b. Flexible configuration
    c. Fast deployment
    d. Rights-based access providing a high level of security
    e. Ability to view invoices in xml format

    Answer: b, c, d

    Explanation:

    Ariba e-Archive:

    - Archive all scanned and electronic invoices
    - Respect tax rules and laws of different countries
        - Retention
        - Archiving
        - Retrieval
    - Advantages
        - Easy access to PDF view of invoices
        - Rights-based access providing a high level of security
        - Efficient and accurate search functions
        - Flexible configuration
        - Fast deployment

    The Ariba Invoicing Solution allows all scanned and electronic invoices to be archived with respect of tax rules and laws of different countries. This includes retention, archiving, and retrieval of invoices.

24. **Which of the following statements are true regarding creating a contract?**

    Please choose the correct answer.

    a. Once the contract workspace has been completed, you must publish the workspace

b. When using Contract Compliance along with Contract Workspaces, it is recommended to have one Contract Workspace template without tasks or documents to simplify the process of creating the Contract Terms document.
c. Both a and b
d. None of the above

Answer: c

Explanation:

Creating a Contract
To create a Contract Terms document within a Contract Workspace, select Actions/Create Contract Terms from the Documents tab of the Workspace. Contract Terms documents can also be created within the template and appear automatically for users.

Depending on the contract workspace template, there may be tasks and documents to complete. When using Contract Compliance along with Contract Workspaces, it is recommended to have one Contract Workspace template without tasks or documents to simplify the process of creating the Contract Terms document. This "Terms Only" workspace is useful when you require the pricing functionality of contracts but do not need the workflow and approval functionality of a workspace.

Once the contract workspace has been completed, you must publish the workspace. When you publish the workspace, Ariba will automatically prompt you to submit the contract terms document (the contract compliance request) for approval.

Creating a Contract

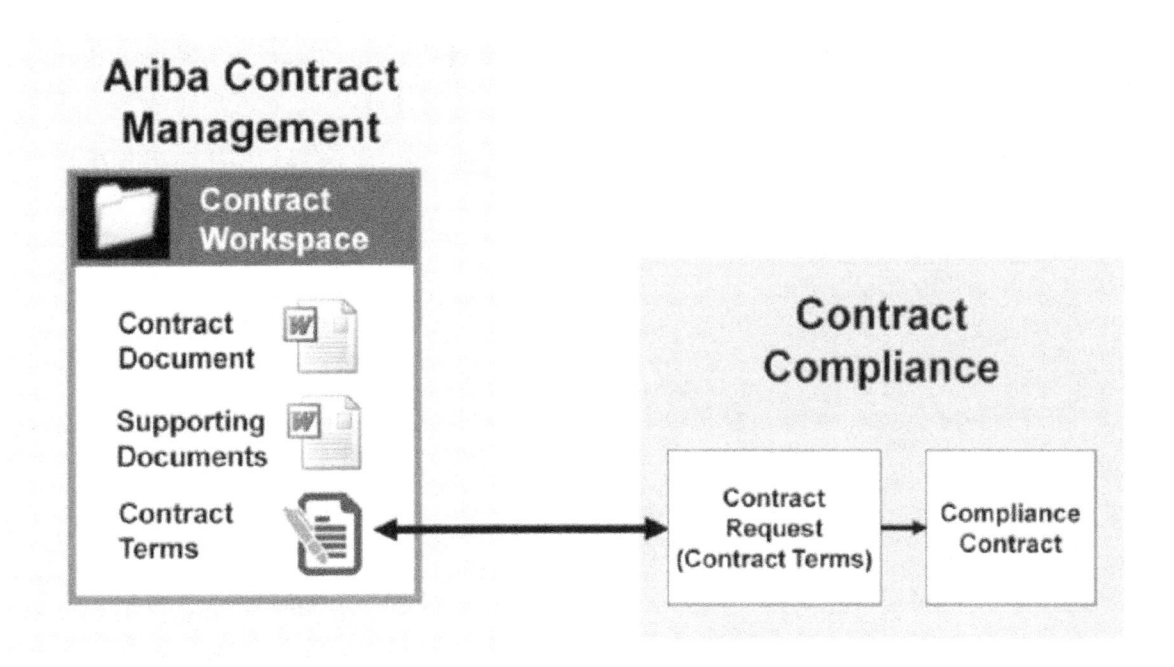

Ariba Contract Management

Contract Workspace
- Contract Document
- Supporting Documents
- Contract Terms

Contract Compliance

Contract Request (Contract Terms) → Compliance Contract

25. **Which of the following statements are true regarding Contract Workspace with Terms?**

    Please choose the correct answer.

    a. When using Contract Workspaces, the contract compliance "Contract Request" becomes a "Contract Terms" document within the Contract Workspace
    b. The Contract Terms document can be created manually or added to the template as a placeholder document which is edited later
    c. Both a and b
    d. None of the above

    Answer: c

    Explanation:

    Contract Workspace with Terms

    When using Contract Workspaces, the contract compliance "Contract Request" becomes a "Contract Terms" document within the Contract Workspace. You can create the Contract Terms on the Documents tab.

    The Contract Terms document can be created manually or added to the template as a placeholder document which is edited later.

Contract Workspace with Terms

- The Contract Compliance document exists as a Contract Terms file on the Documents tab of the Contract Workspace.

- This file can be created from the **Actions** button or it can be built within the Contract Workspace template

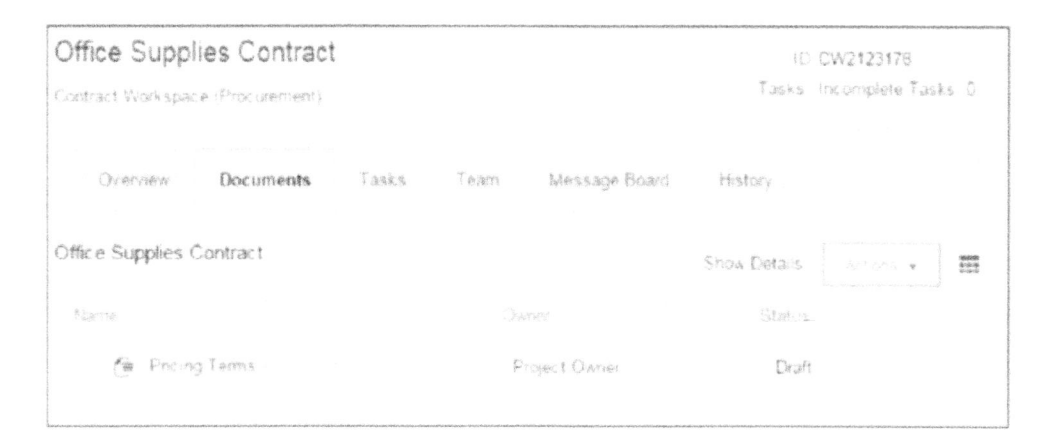

26. The Ariba Commerce Cloud is the most efficient and effective way for organizations to achieve which of the following?

    Note: There are 3 correct answers to this question.

    a. Controlling costs
    b. Minimizing risks
    c. Improving profits
    d. Increasing NPV
    e. Reducing attrition

    Answer: a, b, c

    Explanation:

    The Ariba Commerce Cloud is a web-based platform that enables more efficient and effective global commerce between companies.

    Ariba Commerce Cloud Distinctive Features:
    - On-demand technology to optimize the commerce lifecycle
    - A web-based community to discover, connect, and collaborate with a global network of trading partners

- Capabilities to augment internal resources and skills with always-on expertise and commerce services

The Ariba Commerce Cloud is the most efficient and effective way for organizations to:
- Control costs
- Minimize risks
- Improve profits
- Optimize cash flow
- Increase sales

The Ariba Commerce Cloud

Ariba Sourcing
Ariba Contracts
Ariba Supplier Information and Performance Management

Ariba Procurement
Catalogs
Requisitioning
Ordering
Receiving
Invoicing

Ariba Network
Order and Invoice Transmission
Catalogs
RFX Responses

27. **Which of the following statements are true regarding Ariba Procurement Solution?**

    Note: There are 2 correct answers to this question.

    a. Ariba Procure-to-Order covers all procurement lifecycle processes
    b. Ariba Invoice Pro does not fill the void of inadequate accounts payable automation
    c. Ariba Procurement Content covers some of the Ariba Procure-to-Pay processes, but it uses your ERP system for approvals, creating and sending POs, and receiving and settlement.
    d. Ariba Procure-to-Pay spans the entire lifecycle of a purchasing transaction from requisitioning to ordering to receiving to invoicing and reconciliation.

    Answer: c, d

    Explanation:

Ariba Commerce Cloud and Procurement

Process

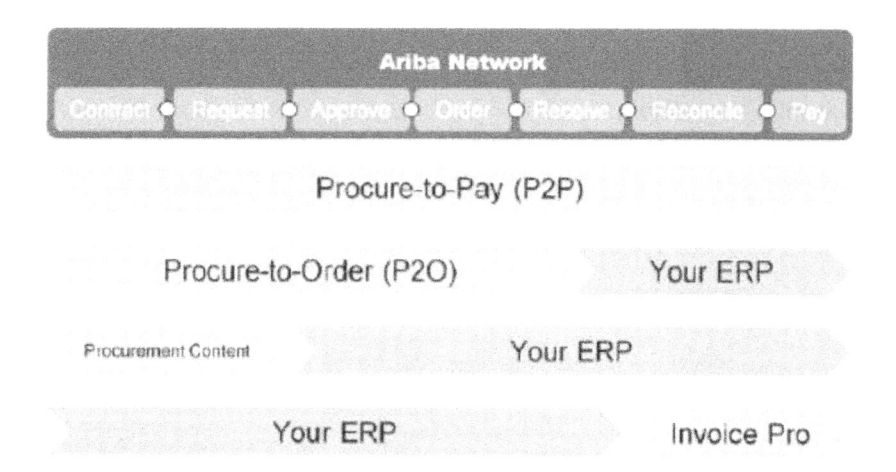

	Ariba Network	
	Contract – Request – Approve – Order – Receive – Reconcile – Pay	

Procure-to-Pay (P2P)

Procure-to-Order (P2O)   Your ERP

Procurement Content   Your ERP

Your ERP   Invoice Pro

Control

Supplier and Contract
- Intuitive shopping
- Compare and collaborate
- Goods and services
- Sustainable catalogs
- Complex contract terms

Process and Regulation
- Approval processes
- Budgets
- Supplier interface
- Receipt management
- Consolidate ERPs

Automation and Payment
- Paperless processing
- Invoice automation options
- Approval matching
- Payment management

Ariba Commerce Cloud and Procurement
The Ariba Commerce Cloud provides strong support for every aspect of procurement and spans the entire commerce lifecycle from sourcing to settlement and from market to receipt. It enables your organization to control the purchasing process through a comprehensive set of features.

Ariba Procurement Solution
- Ariba Procure-to-Pay spans the entire lifecycle of a purchasing transaction from requisitioning to ordering to receiving to invoicing and reconciliation.
- Ariba Procure-to-Order covers most of the procurement lifecycle processes, with the exception of invoice reconciliation and payment.
- Ariba Procurement Content covers some of the Ariba Procure-to-Pay processes, but it uses your ERP system for approvals, creating and sending POs, and receiving and settlement.
- Ariba Invoice Pro fills the void of inadequate accounts payable automation.

28. **To access the Ariba Procurement Solution you need to enter your username and password on a login screen. Your company security and authentication rules govern which of the following three possible login authentication methods?**

Note: There are 3 correct answers to this question.

a. Application authentication
b. Application authentication with Single Sign-On
c. Corporate authentication
d. Corporate authentication with Single Sign-On
e. Corporate authentication with Multiple Sign-On

Answer: a, c, d

Explanation:

To access the Ariba Procurement Solution you need to enter your username and password on a login screen.

Your company security and authentication rules govern which of the following three possible login authentication methods apply:
- **Application authentication:** Users have an Ariba product user names and password that they enter on the Ariba login page. The user names and passwords are maintained by the administrator within the Ariba product.
- **Corporate authentication:** A remote authentication mechanism where users log in to the Ariba product using a user name and password that matches the corporate user name and password.
- **Corporate authentication with Single Sign-On:** A remote authentication mechanism where users log into their corporate network, which automatically logs them in to their Ariba product when needed. Single Sign-On with Corporate Authentication provides benefits to your organization, but requires your network administrators to enable communication between your user authentication system and the Ariba Procurement Solution.

The initial privacy statement needs to be acknowledged the first time a user logs in.

29. **Dashboards can have a maximum of how many tiles?**

Please choose the correct answer.

a. 2
b. 3
c. 4
d. 5
e. 6

Answer: d

Explanation:

Dashboard Tiles:

Tiles sit at the top of your dashboard and display pertinent information. This may include items which require action, small reports, an overview of your approvables, and more.
The tiles are configurable. Click the dropdown arrow on any tile and select **Manage All Tiles** to add or remove tiles from your dashboard. Dashboards can have a maximum of five tiles.

Dashboard Tiles

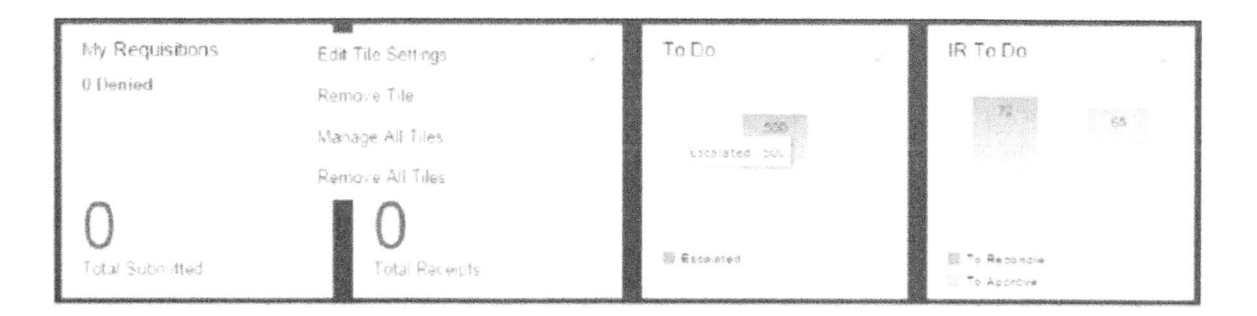

30. How many themes exist for the Ariba user interface?

    Please choose the correct answer.

    a. 2
    b. 3
    c. 4
    d. 5

    Answer: a

    Explanation:

    Ariba Theme:

    The Ariba user interface has two themes: a dark theme and a light theme. You can switch between these themes using the User Preferences menu.

User Preferences

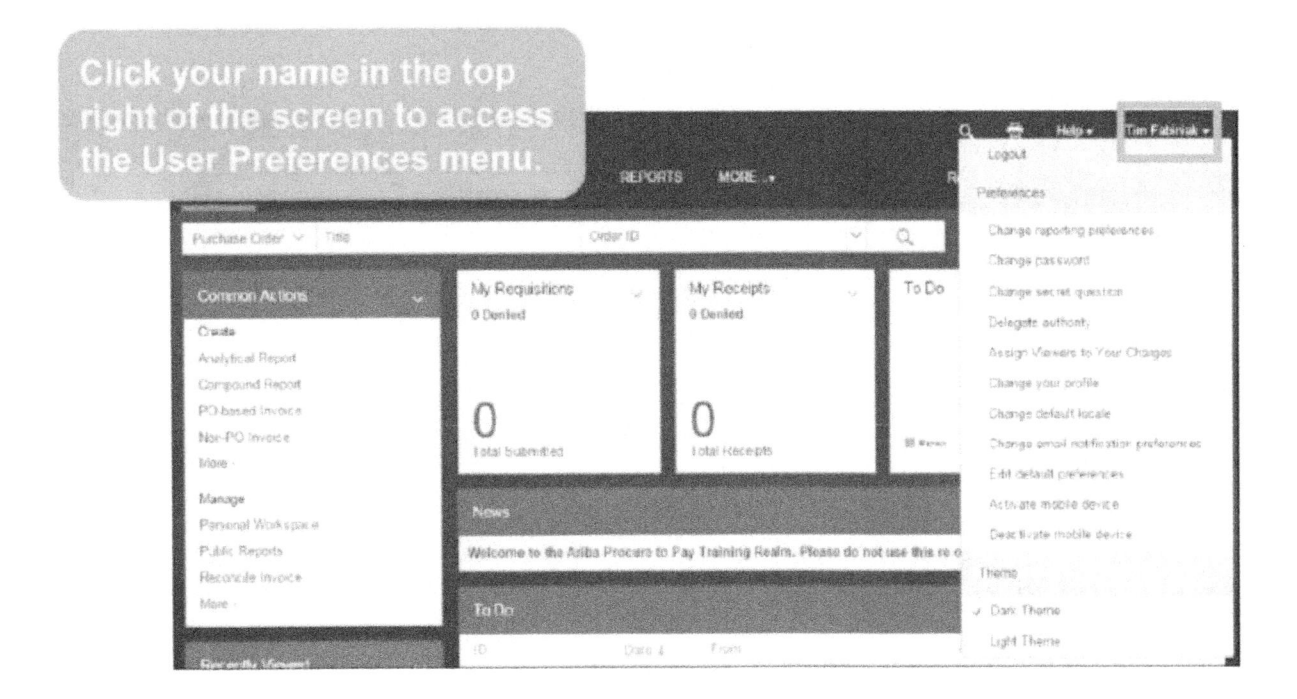

Click your name in the top right of the screen to access the User Preferences menu.

31. **In Catalog Search, Keyword searches default to which of the following searches?**

    Please choose the correct answer.

    a. AND
    b. OR
    c. NOT
    d. None of the above

    Answer: a

    Explanation:

    Search Functionality:

    To search for an exact phrase, use quotation marks around the search terms. For example, if you search for **"USB cable"** the search will only return results with the exact phrase "USB cable."

    Keyword searches default to AND searches. That means that all terms must match an item for that item to be returned. For example, if you search for **USB cable** the search will run as **USB AND Cable.** You can also include the OR keyword; **cable or adapter** will return results with "adapter" in addition to results with "cable". To exclude words from a search, use a leading dash character: **cable -USB** will return results matching "cable" without "USB".

Catalog Search

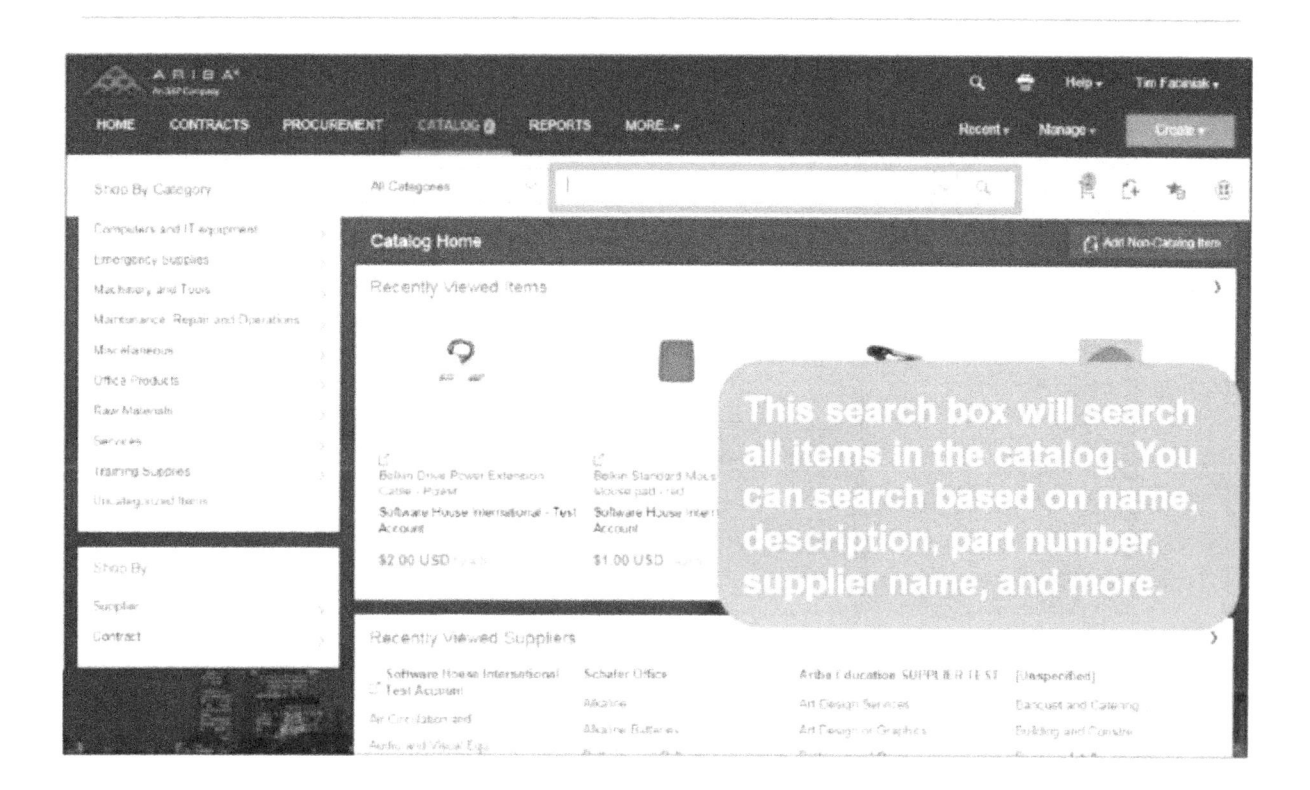

32. **Which of the following statements are true regarding Search functionality in Ariba?**

    Note: There are 2 correct answers to this question.

    a. Ariba will attempt to return results only if the spelling is perfect
    b. Trailing wildcard searching is not automatic for keyword searches
    c. To exclude search options, you need to use a dash
    d. Stemming allows users to search, for example, for either "battery" or "batteries" and find results for both

    Answer: c, d

    Explanation:

Search Functionality

STEMMING

Search for *battery*

Results: *battery batteries*

PARTIAL WORD

Want to search for *polyethylene*

Just type *poly*

BOOLEANS

All terms : **or**
Example: *paper* **or** *plastic bags*

Exclude word (NOT): -
Example: *cable -USB*

FUZZY SPELLING

Search for *Moniter*

Results: *Monitors*

Stem Search
Stemming allows users to search for either "battery" or "batteries" and find results for both.

Partial Word or Wildcard Search
Trailing wildcard searching is automatic (for example, automatically adding "s" or "ing" to the term) for keyword searches. There is no need to search for "polyethylene." A search for "poly" will return results which start with those letters.

Booleans
You can use "or" to search for two options, for example: "paper or plastic bags." To exclude search options, use a dash: "bags -plastic" will return bags without "plastic."

Fuzzy spelling
We are not all spelling bee champions. Ariba will attempt to return results that sound like your search, even if the spelling isn't perfect. "Moniter" returns monitors.

33. **In Ariba, which of the following is the default sorting to sort search results?**

    Please choose the correct answer.

    a. Name

b. Price
c. Relevance
d. Best selling

Answer: c

Explanation:

Sorting Search Results
You can customize search results by modifying the sort order and the level of information that is displayed. These settings will remain in effect until you change them.

Sort By
After search results display, you can choose from four different sort options:
- View the search results by **Relevance** (most popular items first). Relevance is determined based on the number of times an item is ordered.
- View the search results by **Price.**
- View the search results by **Best Selling.**
- View the search results **alphabetically** by Name.

You can sort your search results by:
- Relevance (how closely result matches your search results) - this is the default sorting method
- Price
- Best selling
- Name

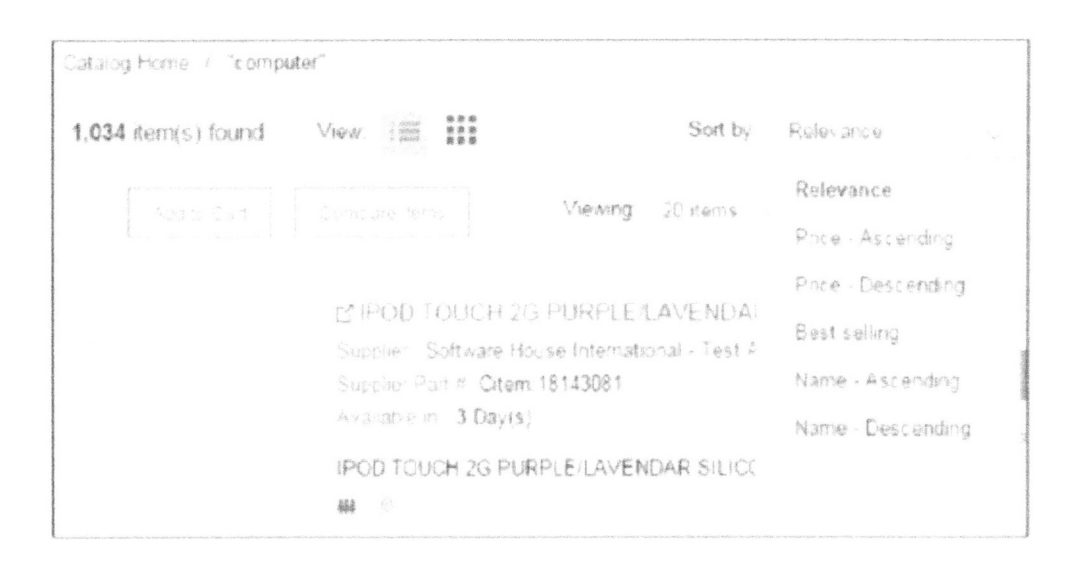

34. **In Ariba, which of the following statements are true regarding Favorite items?**

   Note: There are 3 correct answers to this question.

a. Favorite items cannot be grouped
b. Favorite items are not searchable
c. Catalog Managers can make Public favorites visible to all users or users with a specified group assignment
d. Catalog items that have been assigned to a favorite group are marked with a star when displayed in the catalog.
e. Favorites provide a fast way for users to find products they order frequently

Answer: c, d, e

Explanation:

Favorite Items:

- Favorite items can be grouped
- Favorite items are searchable
- Catalog Managers can make Public favorites visible to all users or users with a specified group assignment

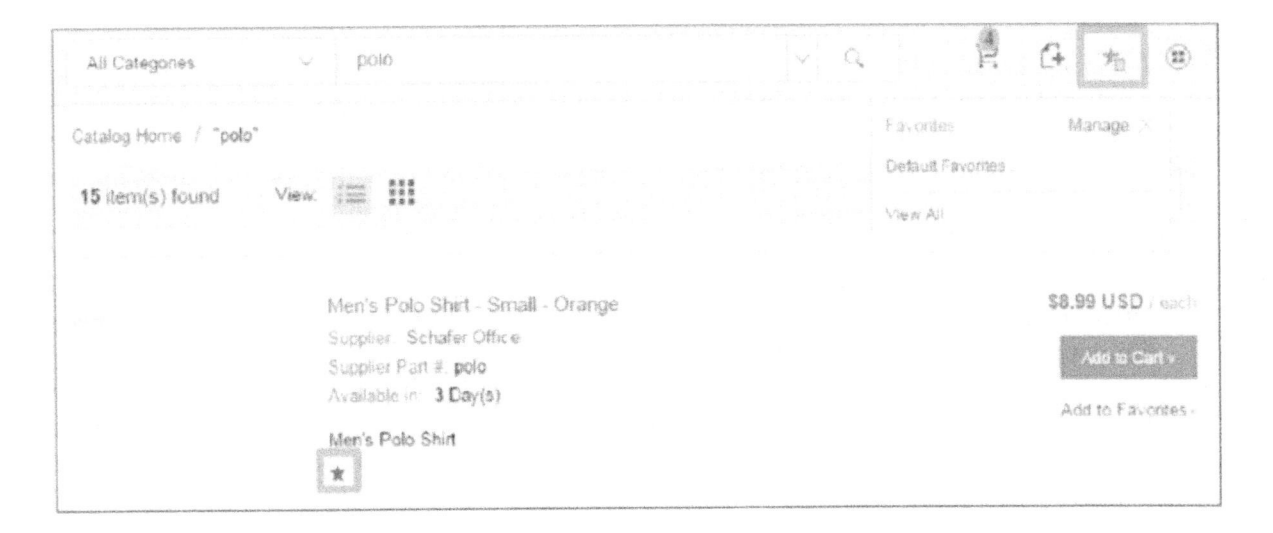

Favorites provide a fast way for users to find products they order frequently. Users create their own Favorites and select as many items as they like. Catalog items that have been assigned to a favorite group are marked with a star when displayed in the catalog.

Users can search for favorite items along with other items in the catalog.

35. **Which of the following statements are true regarding Punchout Catalogs?**

    Note: There are 2 correct answers to this question.

a. The punchout items always behave the same way as catalog items once they have returned to Ariba
b. A punchout session adds items to the shopping cart
c. Punchout allows users to shop for items directly on the supplier's punchout website
d. A supplier can have only one link to the punchout catalog

Answer: b, c

Explanation:

Punchout Catalogs:

- Punchout allows users to shop for items directly on the supplier's punchout website
- A punchout session adds items to the shopping cart
- The punchout items behave the same way as catalog items once they have returned to Ariba with some exceptions
    - For example, to change the quantity or other item information, you must return to the punchout site
    - You must also return to the punchout site to delete some (but not all) of the items
- A supplier can have one link or multiple links to the punchout catalog

A Punchout catalog is a remote catalog hosted by the supplier. The item displayed is presented as a link to the supplier website where the catalog content resides. The user selects the link and the Ariba Procurement Solution displays the supplier's website. The user shops the website, selects (and even configures) desired items, then checks out. The contents of the website's shopping cart is returned to the user's requisition in the Ariba Procurement Solution.

A Punchout session moves a fully configured catalog item to the user's local requisition. The supplier does not take any action other than offer a reservation for the chosen item or service. The supplier does not start fulfillment until an approved purchase order has been received.

Level 1 Punchout suppliers have one Punchout link which displays a store-level view of the catalog. Level 2 Punchout suppliers have multiple Punchout links that display an aisle-level, shelf-level, or item-level view of the catalog.

36. **The Punchout process involves which of the following?**

    Please choose the correct answer.

    a. Buyer
    b. Supplier
    c. Ariba Network
    d. Only b and c
    e. All of the above

    Answer: e

Explanation:

Punchout Process Flow:

The Punchout process involves the buyer, the supplier, and the Ariba Network.
Punchout messages are routed through the Ariba Network for validation and authentication.

1. The user selects a Punchout item in the Ariba Procurement Solution catalog. This selection sends a request to the Ariba Network to establish a connection with the remote catalog.
2. The Ariba Network authenticates the buying organization and forwards the request to the supplier's Punchout site.
3. The supplier sends back a URL of a webpage on the supplier's Punchout site designed specifically for the buyer. The procurement system redirects the user to this URL. The remote shopping site appears in the user's window and the user begins shopping.
4. After shopping, the user clicks the site's **Check Out** button, which moves the contents of the shopping cart from the supplier site back to Ariba Procurement.

Punchout Process Flow

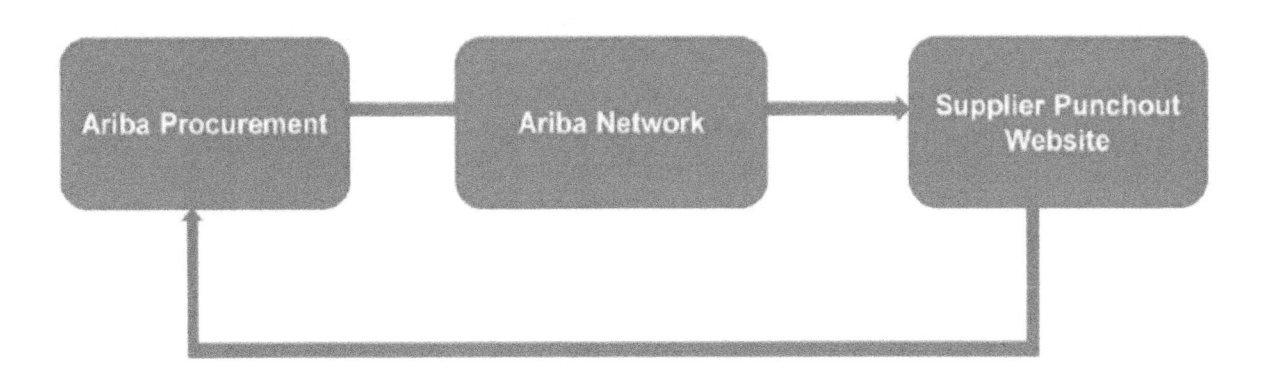

37. **Which of the following statements are true regarding Catalog Kits?**

    Note: There are 2 correct answers to this question.

    a. You can delete items that are marked "required"
    b. Kits are configured by catalog administrators
    c. Enables you to add multiple, bundled products with one mouse click
    d. After adding a kit to a requisition, users will not be able to modify the items

Answer: b, c

Explanation:

Catalog Kits:

The Ariba Procurement Solution supports kits, which are preconfigured groups or bundles of catalog items. They allow users to add commonly needed items or multiple items required for a specific job with just one click.

Kits can contain items from multiple suppliers.

After adding kits to requisitions, users can change values to order different quantities or to delete individual items (if the kit allows this change).

- Enables you to add multiple, bundled products with one mouse click
- Kits are configured by catalog administrators
- After adding a kit to a requisition, users may be able to modify the items (add, delete, or change quantity)
- You cannot delete items that are marked "required"

38. **Which of the following statements are true regarding Catalog Kit Features and Functions?**

    Note: There are 3 correct answers to this question.

    a. A catalog kit is a grouping of items/services as a single catalog entry
    b. Created from existing catalog items
    c. Kits represent groups of items that are frequently purchased together
    d. You can't click a kit name in the catalog to see more information about the kit
    e. When a user adds a kit to a requisition, the system doesn't unbundle it

    Answer: a, b, c

    Explanation:

    Catalog Kit Features & Functions:

    - A catalog kit is a grouping of items/services as a single catalog entry
    - Created from existing catalog items
    - Kits represent groups of items that are frequently purchased together
    - Examples:
        - Retail displays New employee kits
        - Laptop with warranty, bag, and other accessories

    Each kit appears as one item in the catalog. When a user adds a kit to a requisition, the system unbundles it so that each item appears on its own line.

You can click a kit name in the catalog to see more information about the kit, including what items the kit contains, items in the kit that are required, and items that are no longer available (such as items that have expired).

39. **Any type of item can be added to a Catalog kit with certain exception(s). Which of the following is/are the exception(s)?**

    Please choose the correct answer.

    a. Existing kits
    b. Non-catalog items
    c. Punchout items
    d. Only b and c
    e. All of the above

    Answer: e

    Explanation:

    Managing Catalog Kits:

    - Users with the Customer Catalog Manager group create catalog kits
    - Kits are created manually
    - Customer Catalog Manager can request approval of a new kit
    - Any type of item can be added to a kit with the exception of:
        - Existing kits
        - Non-catalog items
        - Punchout items

    Kits are created by catalog administrators and they are available to all end users.

    They allow users to add commonly needed items or multiple items required for a specific job with just one click. Kits can contain items from multiple suppliers.

40. **Which of the following statements are true regarding Kits?**

    Note: There are 2 correct answers to this question.

    a. Kits are a concept available only in the catalog
    b. They can be created by data load
    c. They can be exported
    d. If your organization imports requisitions, those requisitions can contain kits.

    Answer: a, d

Explanation:

Managing Catalog Kits:

Kits are created by catalog administrators and they are available to all end users.

They allow users to add commonly needed items or multiple items required for a specific job with just one click. Kits can contain items from multiple suppliers.

Kits are a concept available only in the catalog; the resulting purchase orders have no mention of kits. They cannot be created by data load and they cannot be exported.

If your organization imports requisitions, those requisitions can contain kits.

41. **In order to start a requisition, how many ways exist?**

    Please choose the correct answer.

    a. 2
    b. 3
    c. 4
    d. 5

    Answer: b

    Explanation:

    There are three ways to start a requisition:
    - Choose **Select Requisition** from the **Create** menu.
    - Search the catalog through the **Search** content item.
    - Browse the Catalog through the **Catalog** tab.

    Any of these options takes you to the Ariba Procurement Solution catalog. Once you add an item to your cart within the catalog, the system will reserve a Requisition number for your use.

Creating a Requisition

```
Creating a Requisition
         ↓
   Add items to your shopping cart
         ↓
   Proceed to checkout
         ↓
   Fill in required Requisition fields
         ↓
   Submit the Requisition for approval
```

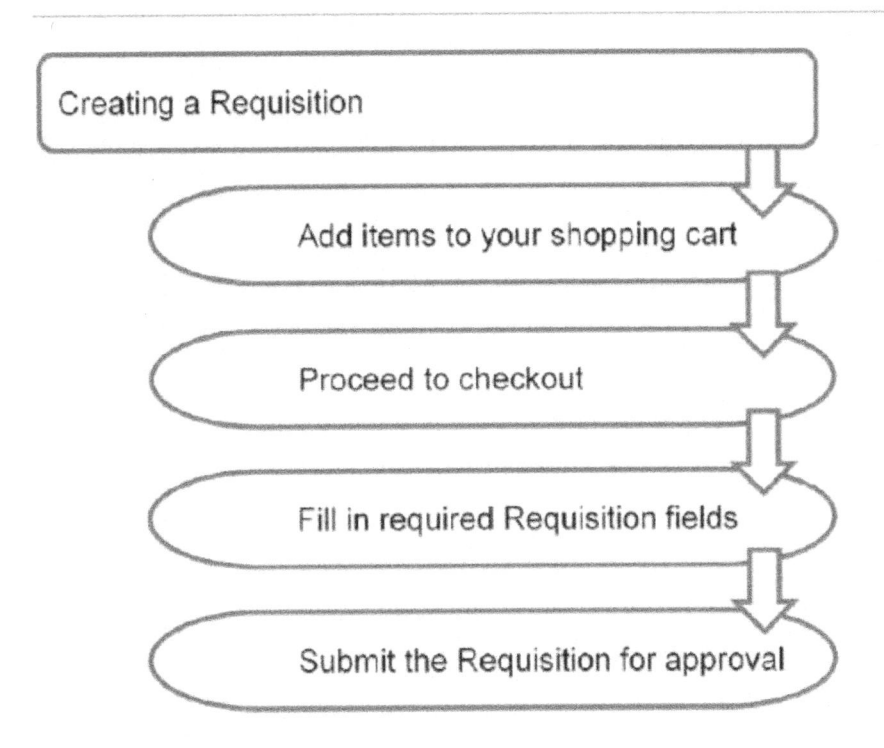

42. **While adding a non-catalog item to a purchase request, the Ariba Procurement Solution prompts you for which of the following mandatory fields?**

    Note: There are 3 correct answers to this question.

    a. Price
    b. Commodity Code
    c. Item Description
    d. Supplier part number
    e. Quantity

    Answer: a, b, c

    Explanation:

    Adding a Non-Catalog Item
    If you cannot find what you are looking for in the catalog, you can add a non-catalog item (also known as an ad hoc item) to your purchase request. You manually enter text to describe these items. The Ariba Procurement Solution prompts you for the price, commodity code, and item description. All other fields are optional.

    To add a non-catalog item:

1. Enter a description for the item.
2. Select a commodity code for the item from the list.
3. Select a supplier from the list. When you select a supplier, the contact field will automatically be filled in. If the name in this field is underlined, you can click it for further details.
4. Enter a price for the item.
5. (Optional) Enter the supplier part number, quantity, and unit of measure if you know these values.
6. Click **OK** to add the item to your requisition.

Requisitions that contain non-catalog items might be routed to your purchasing group, which checks your entries and fills in any missing information after communicating with the supplier.

Adding a Non-Catalog Item

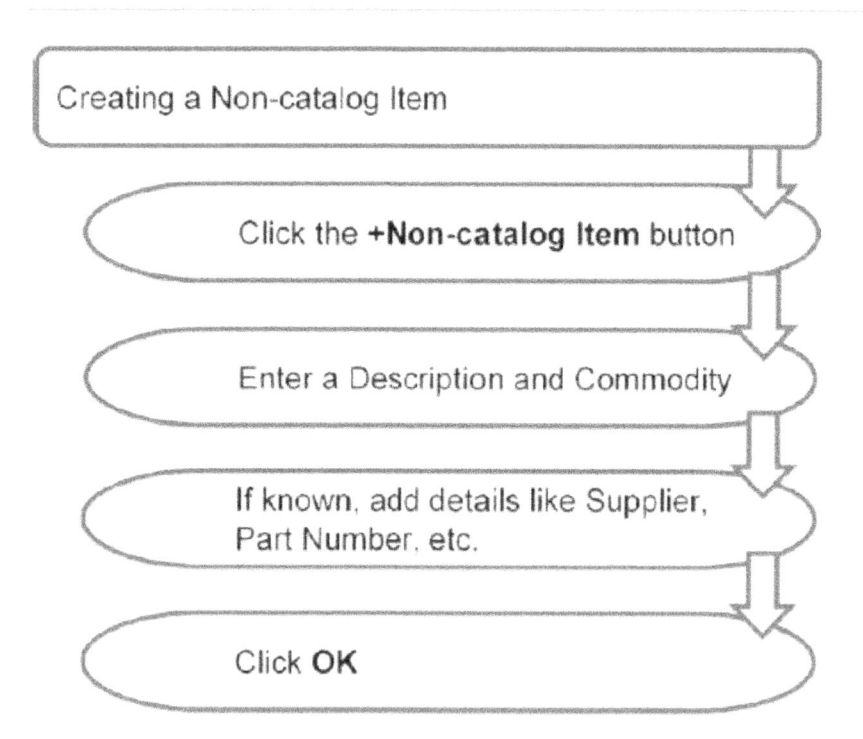

```
Creating a Non-catalog Item
          ↓
Click the +Non-catalog Item button
          ↓
Enter a Description and Commodity
          ↓
If known, add details like Supplier,
Part Number, etc.
          ↓
Click OK
```

43. **Which of the following statements are true regarding Non-catalog items?**

    Note: There are 2 correct answers to this question.

    a. Non-catalog items are generally used for spot-buy items
    b. In general, you should seek to maximize use of non-catalog items
    c. Administrators cannot control which users are allowed to create non-catalog items

d. Non-catalog items can be configured to appear in separate purchase orders from catalog items to streamline supplier fulfillment

Answer: a, d

Explanation:

Adding a Non-Catalog Item:

- Non-catalog items are generally used for spot-buy items
- In general, you should seek to minimize use of non-catalog items:
    - They require review and approval by the purchasing department, and therefore can take longer to approve (and cost more to process)
    - Suppliers often have longer lead times for non-catalog items
- Administrators can control which users are allowed to create non-catalog items.
- Non-catalog items can be configured to appear in separate purchase orders from catalog items to streamline supplier fulfillment.

Minimize the need for non-catalog items by:
- Driving spend to catalogs where possible
- Using item-level contracts to generate catalog subscriptions for items that are standard, but not numerous enough or purchased frequently enough to warrant the supplier furnishing a catalog.
- Generating your own catalog files on behalf of your suppliers to standardize the items.

44. **Ariba uses which of the following to categorize and display products to end users?**

    Please choose the correct answer.

    a. Category code
    b. Display code
    c. Product code
    d. Classification code

    Answer: d

    Explanation:

    Classification Codes:

    - Each product or service must include a classification code
    - Ariba uses this number to categorize and display products to end users
    - Flexible architecture supports all classification codes including UNSPSC and SPSC
    - UNSPSC versioning - You or your suppliers can assign a UNSPSC version number to catalogs

Commodity codes are product or service classification codes, used to group related products together into categories. Each product or service in the catalog must have a commodity code. There are several industry standards for classifying products, such as UNSPSC (United Nations Standard Products and Services Codes).

Ariba provides a flexible architecture that supports transactions using any classification code schema. The Ariba Procurement Solution handles the lack of a consistent standard by allowing each buying organization to choose its own set of commodity coding standard. It uses a set of mapping files to translate the chosen set of commodity codes to other classification schemes on inbound/outbound transactions.

In the default configuration, a subset of the UNSPSC classification code schema is loaded into the application.

45. **Which of the following items need a UOM (Unit of Measure)?**

    Please choose the correct answer.

    a. Catalog items
    b. Non-catalog items
    c. Both a and b
    d. None of the above

    Answer: c

    Explanation:

    Catalog Item Specification: Unit of Measure

    Each catalog and non-catalog item has a unit of measure (UOM), which specifies how that item is shipped, delivered, or packaged. Ariba recommends the use of the UN/CEFACT standard when possible, but provides a flexible architecture that allows other systems such as ANSI/UOM.

    All catalog and non-catalog items need a UOM, which describes how the item is packaged.

    Ariba supports UN/CEFACT and other schemes

UNUOM Code	Meaning
BX	box
DZN	dozen
EA	each
GRO	gross
LBR	pound
RO	roll
PR	pair

Consulting

46. Which of the following should the Customer expect from the CEE (Customer Engagement Executive)?

    Please choose the correct answer.

    a. Advocate
    b. Advisor
    c. Strategist
    d. Only b and c
    e. All of the above

    Answer: e

    Explanation:

    What should the Customer expect from the CEE?

    - Advocate, or the customer within SAP and throughout the life of the relationship
    - Partner, in the development of program goals, scorecard, flight planning, and ongoing stewardship of the program
    - Strategist, that will work with customer and guide project teams to achieve program goals
    - Channel, to the breadth of SAP subject matter experts
    - Advisor, with extensive HR/Procurement LoB experience across a breadth of customer programs and a source for best practices
    - Challenger, to the customer to accomplish more and consider new ways of doing business

    Ariba Governance Structure:

47. **Which of the following person is responsible for Network Growth either regionally or within individual customer accounts?**

   Please choose the correct answer.

   a. Managing Partner
   b. Customer Engagement Manager
   c. Network Growth Manager
   d. Supplier Enablement Lead

   Answer: a

   Explanation:

Program Organization
Comprehensive Roles Descriptions

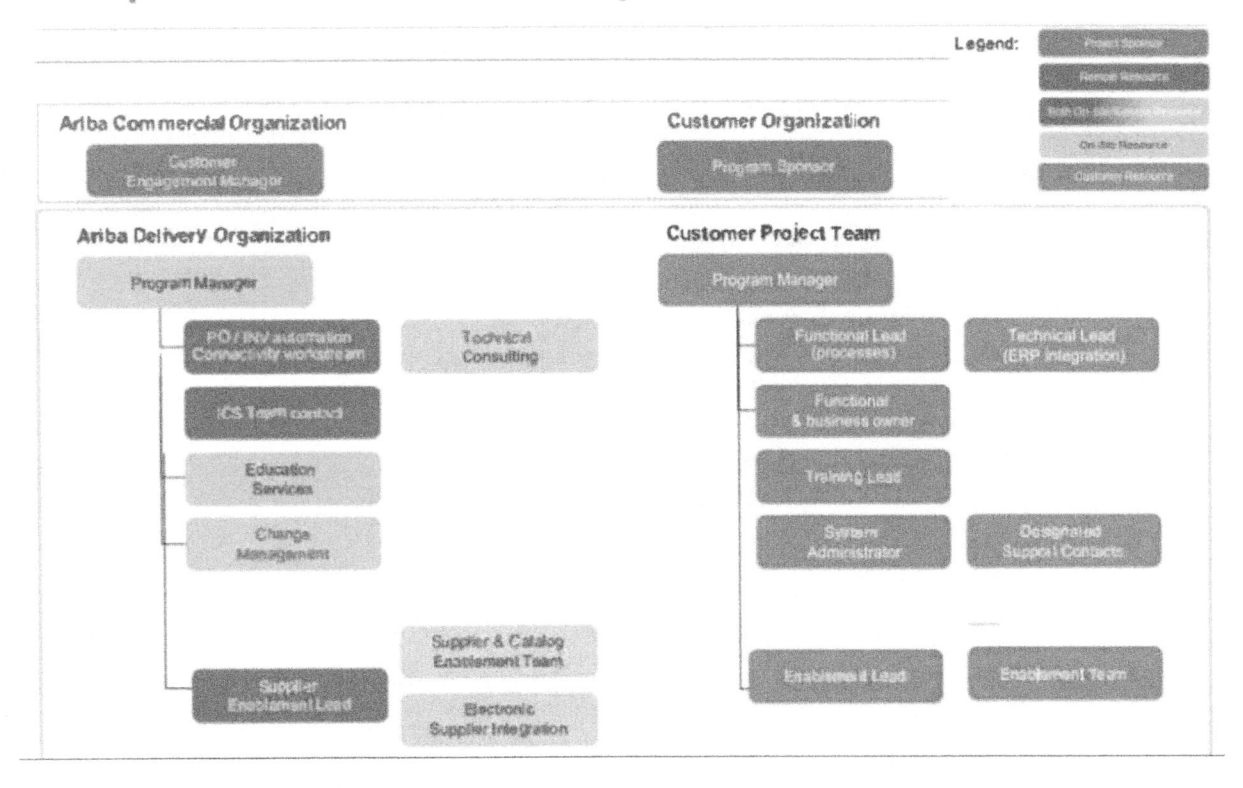

- CEx - Customer Engagement P(Partner), E(Executive), M(Manager)
    - Owns the day to day customer relationship.
- MP/NGP - Managing Partner/Network Growth Partner
    - Responsible for Network Growth either regionally or within individual customer accounts.
- SMP - Supplier Membership Programme
    - Fee structure that generates revenue for Ariba from use of the Ariba Network.
- SMPP - SMP Potential
    - The potential fees derived from a fully-mature supplier on the Ariba Network.
- SMPE - SMP Eligible
    - Point at which suppliers must start paying Ariba Network fees.
- SE Lead - Supplier Enablement Lead
    - Responsible for the execution of Supplier Enablement in new customer programmes.
- NGM - Network Growth Manager
    - Responsible for the execution of Supplier Enablement in existing customer programmes.
- Flight Plan - The operational plan to achieve the customer's programme goals.

48. **Which of the following statement(s) is/are true regarding Flight Plan?**

    Please choose the correct answer.

a. It describes how the Strategy will be implemented
b. It details how the goals will be achieved
c. Both a and b
d. None of the above

Answer: c

Explanation:

What is a Flight Plan?
- Describes how the Strategy will be implemented
    - What suppliers will be approached?
    - How will they be approached?
    - In what order will they be approached and when?
- Details how the goals will be achieved
    - Supplier enablement is not an end in itself
    - It is a process to deliver a clearly defined set of goals

Analyzing Flight Plan Considerations

Spend Characteristic	Favors EARLY Implementation	Favors LATER Implementation	Notes
Amount of addressable spend or volume of transactions	High addressable spend / High transaction volumes	Low addressable spend / Low transaction volumes	Only addressable spend matters, not overall spend.
Potential savings for addressable spend	High potential savings	Low potential savings	Large savings can "fund" later work
Concentration of selected spend	Spend is concentrated in less categories	Spend is not concentrated and spread over many categories	Allows maximum impact with minimal effort
How similar is this region/category	Similar to other regions/categories	Unique, little commonality	Allows reuse of initial work for later categories/regions
Company resource availability to work on project	Sufficient company available resources	Few available company resources	Engage outside consultants if insufficient internal resources

49. Which of the following is not part of high-level process of CCO Flight Planning Tool?

    Note: There are 3 correct answers to this question.

a. Identify Opportunities to Expand Adoption
b. Finalize and Track Progress
c. Review & Refine Flight Plan with customer stakeholders
d. Publish the plan
e. Archive the plan

Answer: a, b, c

Explanation:

Publish the plan is not part of CCO Flight Planning Tool's high-level process.

CCO Flight Planning Tool
High-Level Process

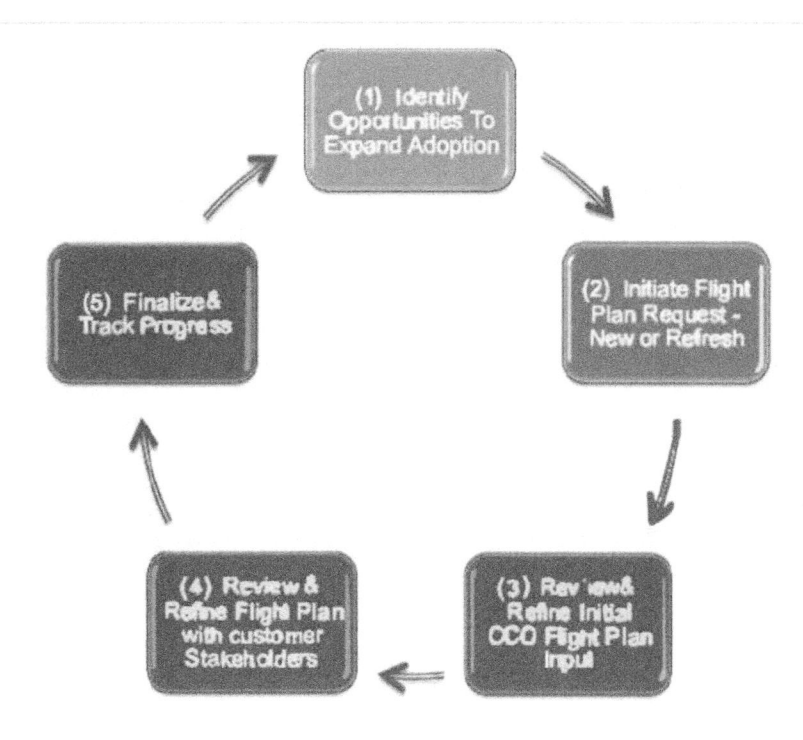

(1) Identify Opportunities To Expand Adoption
(2) Initiate Flight Plan Request – New or Refresh
(3) Review & Refine Initial CCO Flight Plan Input
(4) Review & Refine Flight Plan with customer Stakeholders
(5) Finalize & Track Progress

CCO Flight Planning Tool Methodology

Gather Client Information
- Understand program goals & objectives
- Collect client data
  - Supplier spend
  - Invoice & PO transactions
- Complete questionnaire
- Conduct stakeholder interviews

Perform Data Analysis
- Cleanse and rationalize supplier-level data
- Classify spend & transactions
- Profile suppliers currently on the Ariba Network
- Generate preliminary flight plan based on:
  - Potential savings
  - Ease of implementation
  - Spend
  - Invoice count
  - SMP potential

Validate & Refine Flight Plan with Customer
- Meet with client stakeholders to review preliminary flight plan
- Remove un-addressable categories, suppliers, etc.
- Adjust timing based on client-specific priorities and/or adoption hurdle insights
- Continuous process

50. **Which of the following is/are barrier(s) that need to be removed to accelerate network volume?**

   Please choose the correct answer.

   a. Scenario Gaps
   b. Value & Analysis
   c. Governance
   d. Only a and c
   e. All of the above

   Answer: e

   Explanation:

   Below diagram shows the top 5 barriers that need to be removed to accelerate network volume:

Top 5 Barriers
Remove barriers to accelerate network volume

1. **Governance**
   - Continual stakeholder management, including self services & BPO customers
   - Consistent executive and operational face-off

2. **Documented Best Practices**
   - Assign BTM resources to priority Best Practices
   - Maintain continuity with implementing best practices across accounts

3. **Scenario Gaps**
   - Collaborate to prioritize Scenario gaps
   - Align Documented Best Practices for efficient rollout

4. **Value & Analysis**
   - Create or refresh Business Case, Spend Analysis, Flight Plan. including customer spend
   - Value driven dialog with stakeholders

5. **Backend Complexity**
   - Design Thinking: Simplify backend complexity for Increased Spend Velocity & Lower Enablement Cost
   - Act on high priority recommendations

51. **Which of the following are symptoms of resistance in BTM2 (Business Transformation Management Methodology) - Change Management?**

    Note: There are 2 correct answers to this question.

    a. Lack of abilities
    b. Conflicts
    c. Lack of motivation
    d. Fear of job loss

    Answer: b, c

    Explanation:

    Lack of motivation, Conflicts, Illness, Plots, and Rumors are symptoms of resistances.

The BTM² – Change Management
The psychology of change

> "Factual" argumentation

> Symptoms of resistances
> - Lack of motivation
> - Conflicts
> - Illness
> - Plots
> - Rumours

> Causes for resistances
> - Fear of job loss
> - Lack of abilities
> - Past experiences
> - Values and norms
> - Routine, inflexibility
> - "Not invented here" syndrome

52. Which of the following statements are true regarding BTM² (Business Transformation Management Methodology) - Change Management Approach?

    Note: There are 2 correct answers to this question.

    a. It is targeted to large scale transformations
    b. It provides a comprehensive methodology to deal with changes and the people side in transformation projects
    c. It is based on six steps - doing the right things has the highest priority
    d. It does not provide support to deal with (key) stakeholders, their expectations and potential resistances towards transformation projects

    Answer: a, b

    Explanation:

    The BTM² - Change Management:

    The change management approach . . .
    - is targeted to large scale transformations

- is aligned with the overall BTM2 methodology and phases - envision, engage, transform and optimize
- provides a comprehensive methodology to deal with changes and the people side in transformation projects
- includes "best of breed" knowledge and experiences in the field of organizational psychology, organizational behavior and human resource management
- is based on five steps - doing the right things has the highest priority
- provides support to deal with (key) stakeholders, their expectations and potential resistances towards transformation projects

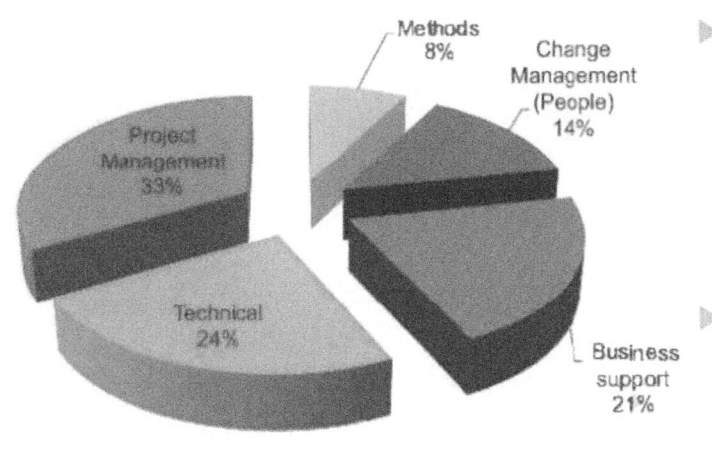

▶ **75% are failing because of non-technical reasons**
e.g. non acceptance of the solution, skill problems, communication problems, problems with project resources

▶ **25% Failure because of technical reasons**
e.g. demands can not be mapped, sizing problems, problems with connecting legacy systems

Pie chart: Project Management 33%, Technical 24%, Business support 21%, Change Management (People) 14%, Methods 8%

53. **Prior to making significant new investments, companies want to understand which of the following?**

   Please choose the correct answer.

   a. Scope of the proposed solution
   b. Improve business intelligence
   c. Realize Return on Investment
   d. Only a and c
   e. All of the above

   Answer: e

   Explanation:

   Business Transformation: Turning Vision into Reality:

   Prior to making significant new investments companies want to understand:

   - The business value and justification
   - Scope of the proposed solution
   - How the solution will enable corporate strategy

- Increase profitability and productivity
- Improve business intelligence
- Realize Return on Investment

Ariba Maturity and Level of Adoption:

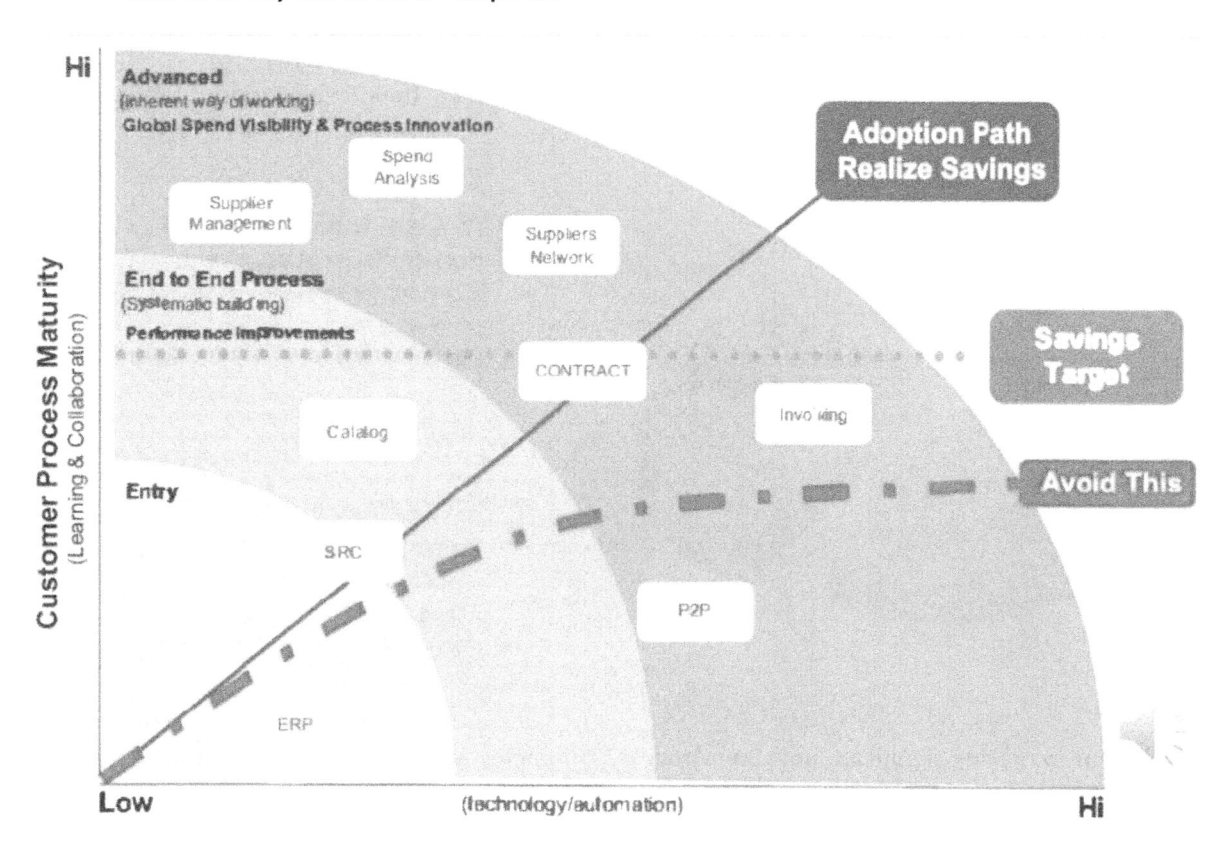

54. **Which of the following are the Success Metrics for Process Improvement?**

    Note: There are 2 correct answers to this question.

    a. Transaction Cycle Times
    b. Visibility of Spend
    c. Maverick Spend
    d. Spend on Catalog

    Answer: a, b

    Explanation:

    Transaction Cycle Times, Electronic Transactions, Visibility of Spend, Suppliers under Management, and Supplier Performance are metrics for Process Improvement.

Success Metrics

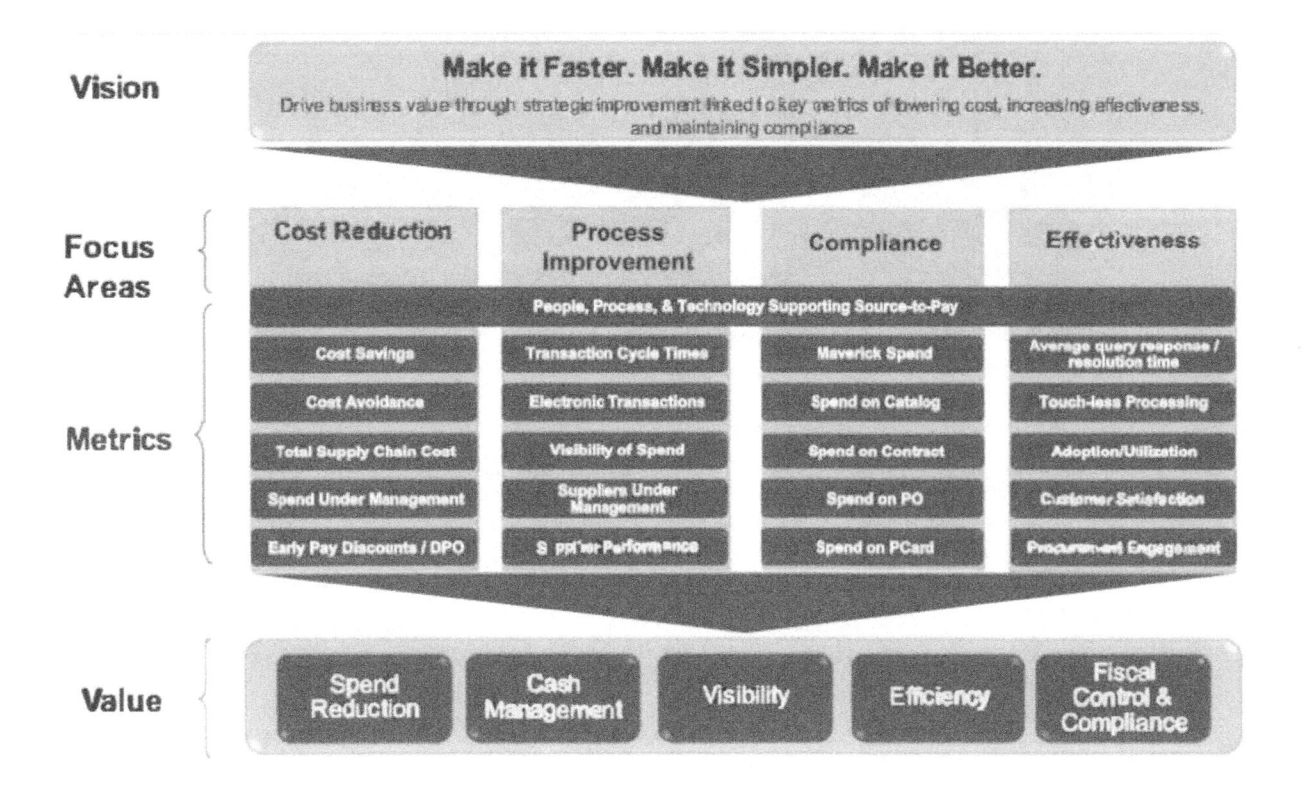

Vision — Make it Faster. Make it Simpler. Make it Better.
Drive business value through strategic improvement linked to key metrics of lowering cost, increasing effectiveness, and maintaining compliance.

Focus Areas: Cost Reduction | Process Improvement | Compliance | Effectiveness

People, Process, & Technology Supporting Source-to-Pay

Metrics:
- Cost Savings | Transaction Cycle Times | Maverick Spend | Average query response / resolution time
- Cost Avoidance | Electronic Transactions | Spend on Catalog | Touch-less Processing
- Total Supply Chain Cost | Visibility of Spend | Spend on Contract | Adoption/Utilization
- Spend Under Management | Suppliers Under Management | Spend on PO | Customer Satisfaction
- Early Pay Discounts / DPO | Supplier Performance | Spend on PCard | Procurement Engagement

Value: Spend Reduction | Cash Management | Visibility | Efficiency | Fiscal Control & Compliance

---

55. **Which of the following are the milestones in Architect Phase of Ariba Methodology?**

    Note: There are 2 correct answers to this question.

    a. Solution Scope Defined
    b. All Project Resources Assigned
    c. System Test Complete
    d. Ready to Migrate to Prod

    Answer: a, b

    Explanation:

    Goals and Objectives Defined, Solution Scope Defined, All Project Resources Assigned, Deployment Project Plan is Completed, Ready to Kick Off, and Deployment Kick off Complete are the milestone in Architect Phase.

The Milestones: Architect Phase

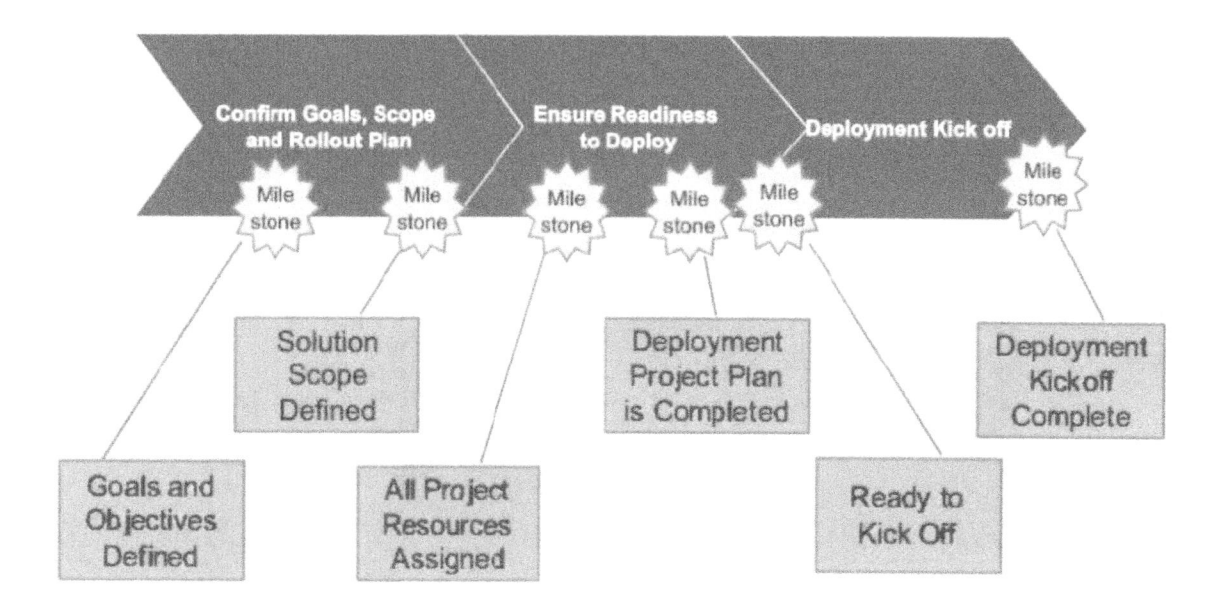

Flow: Confirm Goals, Scope and Rollout Plan → Ensure Readiness to Deploy → Deployment Kick off

Milestones:
- Goals and Objectives Defined
- Solution Scope Defined
- All Project Resources Assigned
- Deployment Project Plan is Completed
- Ready to Kick Off
- Deployment Kickoff Complete

56. **Which of the following statement(s) is/are true regarding Supplier Enablement?**

    Please choose the correct answer.

    a. It is an internal IT Project that just requires the installation and configuration of a piece of technology by a limited part of the business, whilst everything else remains the same
    b. Supplier Enablement will fundamentally change a business forever
    c. Both a and b
    d. None of the above

    Answer: b

    Explanation:

    What is Supplier Enablement?

    Supplier Enablement IS:
    A cross-functional business change programme whereby both buyers and suppliers move away from paper-based processes to an electronic end-to-end business relationship that delivers defined business benefits but requires fundamental shifts in attitudes and processes and a refocus of resources and priorities.

    Supplier Enablement IS NOT:

An internal IT Project that just requires the installation and configuration of a piece of technology by a limited part of the business, whilst everything else remains the same.

Supplier Enablement will fundamentally change a business forever.

Supplier Management Organisation (SMO)

Ariba's Dedicated Team of 200+ Global Professionals

SE Lead / Network Growth Manager	Works with Buying Organisations to deliver successful Supplier Enablement Programmes
Strategic Supplier Account Manager (SSAM)	Works with Strategic Suppliers to deliver successful Collaborative Commerce Programmes
Supplier Manager (SM)	"Start" enablement using SE Automation, track progress, and educate Suppliers in multiple languages
Supplier Manager Liaison (SIL)	Interface between Supplier Managers and the SE Lead / Network Growth Manager
Electronic Supplier Integration Manager (ESIM)	Technical contact for EDI/cXML relationships to support integration to the Ariba Network, provide supplier consulting services and technical support
Catalogue Enablement	Work with suppliers to enable catalogues and provide ongoing catalogue maintenance

57. **On Buy Side, what benefits can be realized through the Ariba Network?**

    Note: There are 2 correct answers to this question.

    a. Lower Processing Costs
    b. Increase Wallet Share
    c. Lower DSO
    d. Mitigate Supply Risk

    Answer: a, d

    Explanation:

    Ariba Network:

    Why should companies adopt the Ariba Network?

- Increasingly, competition is occurring between supply chains & business networks rather than between companies
- Buyers face increasing network complexity and accelerated speed of business: Sellers face increasing customer expectations and customer power
- More agility than ever is needed to adapt to changing markets
- Strong business networks can create competitive advantage and help organizations grow top-line and save on the bottom-line simultaneously

How can SAP help?

- Easy and fast onboarding process
- Huge percentage of business partners already on the network
- Support broad functional areas (E2E processes)
- Integration into SAP backend (MM/SRM)
- Enable customers to pursue SINGLE network strategy

What benefits can be realized?

- Buy Side: Lower Processing Costs (AP and Procurement), Increase Compliance, Mitigate Supply Risk, Maximize Payables Cash Returns
- Sell Side: Increase Wallet Share, Lower Processing Costs (fulfillment, A/R, sales), Lower DSO, Get New Business

58. **Which of the following Contract Workspace type is used for contracts within companies or organizations?**

    Please choose the correct answer.

    a. Contract Workspace (Procurement)
    b. Contract Workspace (Sales)
    c. Contract Workspace (Internal)
    d. Contract Workspace (Company)

    Answer: c

    Explanation:

    Who Can Create a Contract Workspace?
    - Only users with proper system permissions have the ability to create contract workspaces.
        - Menu options based on your permissions
    - System permissions are granted by your system administrator

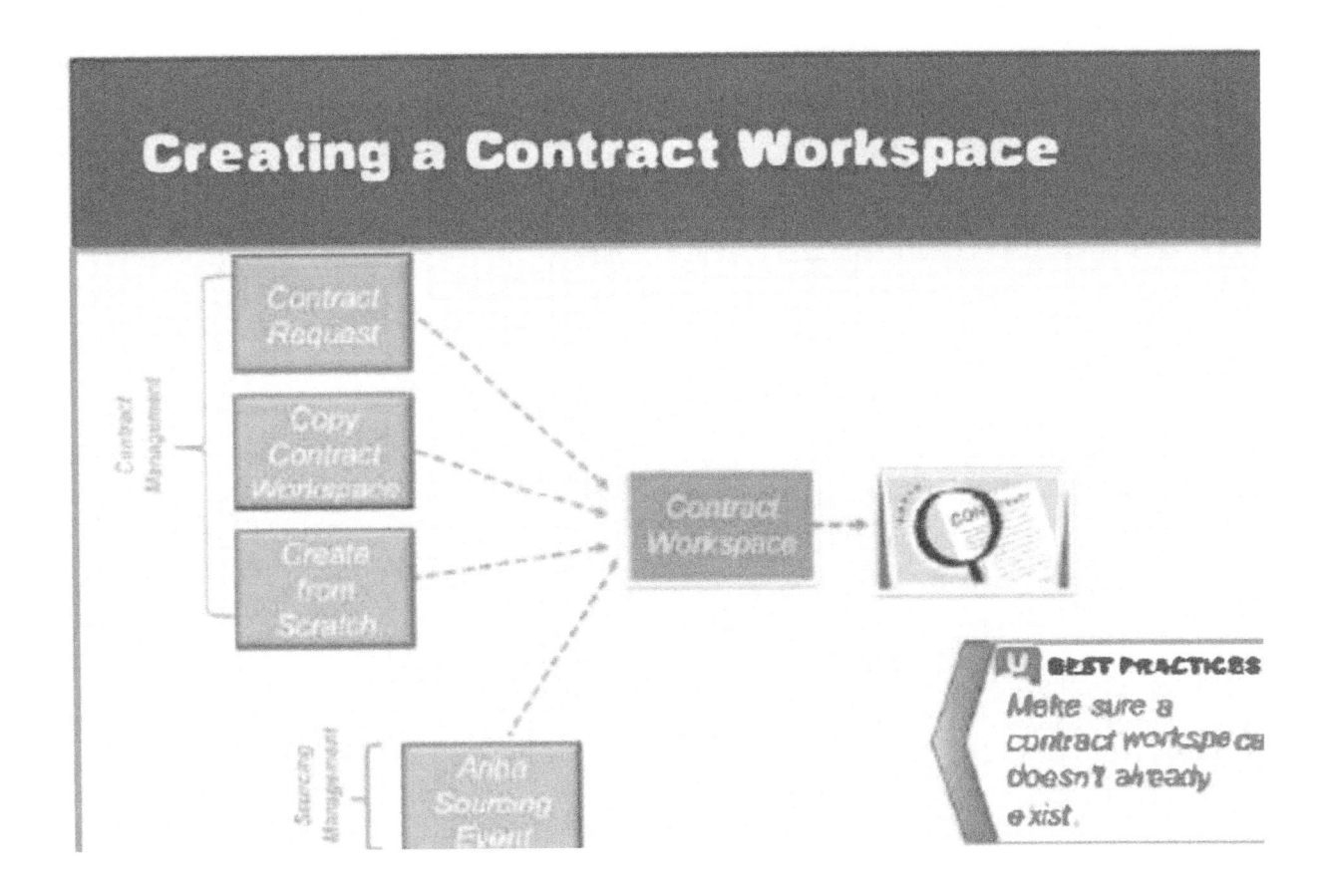

Creating a Contract Workspace

[Diagram showing Contract Management sources (Contract Request, Copy Contract Workspace, Create from Scratch) and Sourcing Management source (Ariba Sourcing Event) all feeding into a Contract Workspace.]

BEST PRACTICES
Make sure a contract workspace doesn't already exist.

Contract Workspace Types:
- Contract Workspace (Procurement)
    - Used for contracts with a supplier
- Contract Workspace (Sales)
    - Used for contracts with a customer or buyer
- Contract Workspace (Internal)
    - Used for contracts within companies or organizations

59. **Which of the following is NOT a Contract Workspace Component?**

Please choose the correct answer.

a. Documents
b. Tasks
c. Overview
d. Team
e. None of the above

Answer: e

Explanation:

A contract workspace is a place to store all your: documents, tasks and due dates, list of team members who will help you create the contract.

Contract Workspace Components

- Overview: contains basic information
- Documents
- Tasks
- Team
- Contract Attributes and Contract Term Attributes

60. Which of the following are the types of tasks in Ariba Contract Management?

    Note: There are 3 correct answers to this question.

    a. To do task
    b. Notification task
    c. Negotiation task
    d. Item to do task
    e. Deletion task

    Answer: a, b, c

    Explanation:

A contract workspace is a place to store all your: documents, tasks and due dates, list of team members who will help you create the contract.

Task:

- Something that needs to be done
    - By a specific person
    - By a specific time
- Can be part of phases
- Can be optional or required
- Can contain predecessor
    - Task/Phase cannot be started until all predecessor tasks have been completed

Types of Tasks in Ariba Contract Management:

- To do task
- Document to do task
- Review / Approval / Negotiation task
    - Tasks that include routing for a document for review, approval or negotiation
    - Allows task owner to create a list of reviewers, approvers
    - Allows reviewers / approvers to add additional approval flow, submit comments, and attachments
- Notification Task

61. **Which of the following statements are true regarding Contract Addendum?**

Please choose the correct answer.

a. It is a Microsoft Word document that contains the text of the Contract Agreement
b. It is organized into Sections and Clauses
c. It provides Microsoft Word integration
d. Only a and c
e. All of the above

Answer: e

Explanation:

Main Agreement or Contract Addendum:

The main Agreement or Contract Addendum is:
- Microsoft Word document that contains the text of the Contract Agreement
- Organized into Sections and Clauses
- Provides Microsoft Word integration:
    - Automatic population of contract fields
    - Outline view
    - Tracking of changes
    - Detailed version comparison

The main agreement and contract addenda documents can be viewed in two ways:
- Microsoft Word
- Outline View in Ariba Contract Management

The assembled document is divided into separate sections and clauses.

Users can access the Clause Library and easily add I substitute clauses.

62. **If the effective date is in the future, the status of the Contract Workspace will be which of the following?**

Please choose the correct answer.

a. Published
b. Pending
c. On Hold
d. Draft

Answer: b

Explanation:

Publishing a Contract Workspace:

- Final step in the contract creation process
- Freezes current version of the Contract Workspace so no further editing is possible
- Only available if all required tasks are completed (Completed/Reviewed/Approved)

Contract 'Published' Status:

Once all required tasks are completed, the owner will publish the Contract Workspace from the Attributes sections. The status of the Contract Workspace will change to either Published or Pending.

The status will be Published if the Effective Date is the current date or earlier.

The status will be 'Pending' if the Effective Date is in the future. When the Effective Date is reached, the status will automatically change to 'Published'.

63. **Which of the following is NOT a Contract status?**

    Please choose the correct answer.

    a. Expired
    b. Draft Amendment
    c. Draft
    d. Deleted

    Answer: d

    Explanation:

    All Contract Statuses:

    - Draft - Currently being worked on and not yet final.
    - Pending - Approved, but the effective date is in the future.
    - Published - Currently effective.
    - Expired - Past the expiration date.
    - On Hold - Suspended (actions are limited)
    - Closed - Manually closed by a user.
    - Draft Amendment - An Amendment that is currently being worked on and not yet final.

64. **Which of the following statements are true regarding Ariba Spend Visibility?**

    Please choose the correct answer.

    a. Includes data enrichment services, where Ariba provides extensive and flexible reporting capabilities
    b. Is an on-demand solution, meaning Ariba hosts and manages the application for you

c. Aggregates, cleans, organizes, and validates your data so your reports are based on better data
d. Only b and c
e. All of the above

Answer: e

Explanation:

The Ariba Spend Visibility Professional solution is a web-based tool that allows analysts to create and manage reports that provide a comprehensive view of spend data across the entire organization.

Ariba Spend Visibility:
- Includes data enrichment services, where Ariba provides extensive and flexible reporting capabilities
- Is an on-demand solution, meaning Ariba hosts and manages the application for you
- Aggregates, cleans, organizes, and validates your data so your reports are based on better data
- Adds commodity classification and supplier enrichment to provide better visibility into your spend.

Ariba Spend Visibility Professional

Provides a comprehensive view of spend across the entire organization which drives business decisions and priorities regarding spend and sourcing opportunities.

Consists of both Ariba services and software.

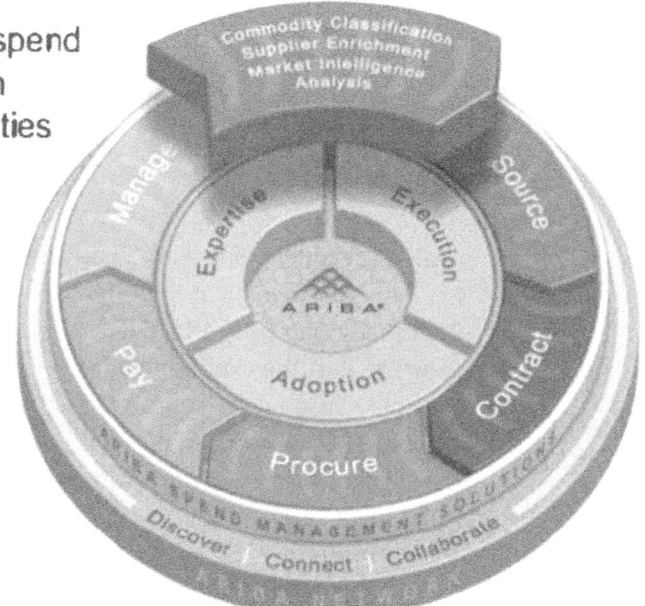

Integration & Forms

65. **Which of the following are ways to create contract requests?**

    Note: There are 3 correct answers to this question.

    a. Create directly
    b. Create from a Contract Workspace
    c. Upload from a Microsoft Excel template
    d. Upload from a PDF
    e. Upload directly

    Answer: a, b, c

    Explanation:

    Creating Contract Requests:

    Creating directly
    Users may be granted access to create contract compliance requests directly using the contract compliance feature of their Ariba Procurement or Invoice solution.

    Creating from a Contract Workspace
    When contract compliance is integrated with Ariba Contract Management, users can create contract compliance requests as part of a contract workspace. Contracts and contract compliance requests can be created, changed, or submitted from the workspace.

    In this scenario, the Contract Terms document serves as the contract compliance request. Typically, the approval flow is automatic and approval is handled by tasks in the contract workspace.

    Uploading from Excel
    Users can create new contract compliance requests by uploading a Microsoft Excel file containing the contract terms and pricing information. The spreadsheet used for this purpose must match the required format. The recommended way to begin this process is to export an existing compliance contract to Microsoft Excel. This file can then be used as the starting point for creating a new contract request.

Creating Contract Requests

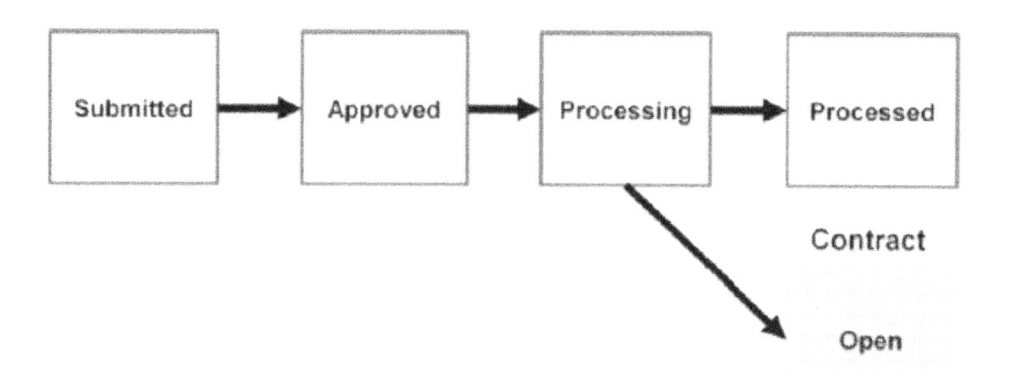

```
Submitted → Approved → Processing → Processed
                            ↓         Contract
                           Open
```

- Create directly
- Create from a Contract Workspace (as the Contract Terms document)
- Upload from a Microsoft Excel template

66. **Which of the following statements are true regarding Release Order Contracts?**

    Note: There are 3 correct answers to this question.

    a. Does not support standard procurement functionality
    b. Allow certain users direct release access
    c. Automatically attach to requisitions
    d. Automatically adjust accumulators
    e. Does not allow purchases to be made against a contract

    Answer: b, c, d

    Explanation:

    Release Order Contracts:

    - A release order is a purchase order associated with a contract
    - Allow purchases to be made against a contract
    - Automatically adjust accumulators
    - Support standard procurement functionality
    - Automatically attach to requisitions
    - Allow certain users direct release access

In the contract request wizard the **Release Required** field determines whether or not the contract will require release orders.

Release order contracts match pricing terms to items added to requisitions so that release orders (purchase orders associated to the contract) are generated against the contract.

Some of the key features of release order contracts include:
- **Automatic adjustment of accumulators**
  As release orders consume funds on the contract, contract compliance automatically adjusts the accumulators which track values such as the available amount left on the contract.
- **Standard procurement functionality**
  This type of contract supports functionality such as change orders and line item split accounting.
- **Automatic attachment to requisitions**
  When a user selects an item that is covered by a contract, the system can automatically attach the contract to the requisition.
- **Direct release access**
  Certain users may be granted access to select items directly from the contract (rather than from the catalog) to generate release orders.

67. **Which of the following statements are true regarding No-release Order Contracts?**

    Note: There are 2 correct answers to this question.

    a. Allow contract purchase orders
    b. Allow direct receiving and invoicing
    c. Does not provide additional pricing terms
    d. Can be used for bookkeeping purposes when direct receiving and invoicing have been disabled

    Answer: b, d

    Explanation:

    No-release Order Contracts:

    - Does not allow contract purchase orders
    - Allow direct receiving and invoicing
    - Provide additional pricing terms:
        - Fixed and recurring fee items
        - Costs
        - Expenses
    - Can be used for bookkeeping purposes when direct receiving and invoicing have been disabled

Contracts that do not require release orders are referred to as no-release order contracts. This type of contract does not allow release/purchase orders, but includes other functionality to address non-PO based types of purchasing.

Direct receiving and invoicing- Since purchase orders are not allowed, there are options to enable direct receiving and invoicing. This allows the system to capture information used to match against the terms of the contract even in the absence of purchase orders.

Pricing terms- This type of contract supports more than just the materials and services pricing terms available in release order contracts. These include fixed/recurring fees, costs, and expenses.

Aggregating sub agreements- You can also use a no-release order contract to aggregate the orders and invoices for other contracts. For example, you may have multiple regional contracts with the same supplier. However, you want to easily see the aggregated orders and invoices from all of the regional contracts. A no release order contract could be the parent of each of the sub agreement regional contacts, aggregating all of the information from the sub agreement regional release order contracts.

68. **Which of the following statements are true regarding Blanket Purchase Orders (BPOs) in Ariba?**

    Note: There are 2 correct answers to this question.

    a. BPOs must have a maximum amount
    b. BPO spend is accrued on the invoice date
    c. BPOs are created through the Requisition creation process
    d. BPOs are sent to the supplier through the Ariba Network as a PO and will appear in the supplier's Inbox, both as a Contract and as a Purchase Order

    Answer: a, d

    Explanation:

    Blanket Purchase Orders in other systems:

    - Blanket Purchase Orders may be created through a requisition process by swapping dollar and quantity values
    - The BPO is used to allocate funds for repeated purchases
    - Terms of the BPO are created once only on the BPO
    - The invoice may be created directly against the PO

    Blanket Purchase Orders in Ariba:

    - The functionality above is part of our standard Contract behavior with no need for dollar/quantity swapping
    - BPOs are a subtype of Contracts, both Release and No-release, with a few small changes:
        - BPOs must have a maximum amount

- o BPO spend is accrued on the contract affective date, not on the order or invoice date
- o BPOs are sent to the supplier through the AN as a PO and will appear in the supplier's Inbox, both as a Contract and as a Purchase Order
- BPOs are created through the Contract creation process, not the Requisition creation process, and follow the Contract Request approval flow

69. **Which of the following statements are true regarding Discount Pricing?**

    Note: There are 2 correct answers to this question.

    a. Discounted Price is used with all contract types
    b. Discount Percent is used only for item-level contracts
    c. Discount Percent can be used with both catalog and non-catalog items
    d. Discounted Price can be used with only catalog items
    e. Discounted Price set the price of the item

    Answer: c, e

    Explanation:

    Discount Pricing:

    Only item level contracts can use pricing structures that are based on quantity or indicate a specific discounted price.

    Discount Pricing:
    Only *Volume Discounts - Per Order at* the Supplier and Commodity Code level are not supported. This is due to the fact that it is unknown during requisitioning which line items will be combined into one order.

    Users can specify discount pricing for a supplier, commodity, catalog, or non-catalog item. Flat discounts can be defined in one of two ways:
    - Based on a specified **price** which includes the discount
    - Based on a specific **percentage** which is used to discount the regular price

    A discounted price can be applied to catalog and non-catalog items only. A fixed percentage off can be applied to catalog items, commodities, or all items offered by a supplier.

Discount Pricing

Discounted Price
- Only for item-level contracts
- Can be used with both catalog and non-catalog items
- Set the price of the item

Discount Percent
- Used with all contract types
- Can be used with both catalog and non-catalog items

70. **To create contract hierarchies, you select the proper hierarchical type in the contract request wizard or in the contract workspace. Which of the following are the choices available?**

    Note: There are 3 correct answers to this question.

    a. Standalone agreement
    b. Master agreement
    c. Sub agreement
    d. Multi-level agreement
    e. Multi-task agreement

    Answer: a, b, c

    Explanation:

    Contract Hierarchies:

```
        ┌──────────────┐
        │    Master    │
        │   Agreement  │
        │              │
        │ Supplier level│
        │   contract   │
        └──────────────┘
           ▲
    ┌──────┴──────┐
┌─────────────┐ ┌─────────────┐
│Subagreement │ │Subagreement │
│             │ │             │
│ Item level  │ │Commodity level│
│  contract   │ │  contract   │
└─────────────┘ └─────────────┘
                       ▲
                ┌─────────────┐
                │Subagreement │
                │             │
                │ Item level  │
                │  contract   │
                └─────────────┘
```

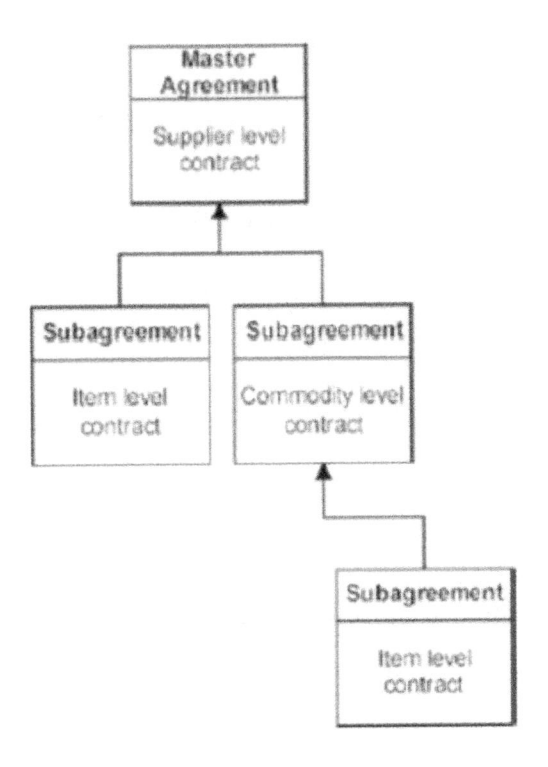

A contract hierarchy is a set of related contracts that can share accumulated amounts and pricing discounts. Hierarchies allow users to better track and manage multi-level, complex vendor agreements. Users have visibility to spend at the master agreement level (as an aggregate), as well as at individual sub agreement levels. Hierarchies are also useful for agreements with different pricing types, such as a discounted price on specific items and a flat discount on everything else.

To create contract hierarchies, you select the proper hierarchical type in the contract request wizard or in the contract workspace. The choices are:

- **Standalone agreement** - this type of contract cannot be part of a hierarchy.
- **Master agreement** - the top level of a contract hierarchy. To create a contract hierarchy, you must begin by designating a master agreement.
- **Sub agreement** - an agreement that has a parent agreement in a contract hierarchy.

The diagram depicts a basic contract hierarchy. The master agreement is at the top level of the hierarchy. Each contract can have only one parent, but can have as many sub agreements as necessary.

You cannot specify a parent agreement that is more specific than the sub agreement. For example, an item-level contract could not be referenced as the parent of a commodity-level agreement.

71. Which of the following statements are true regarding Compound Pricing?

    Note: There are 2 correct answers to this question.

    a. The calculation for compound pricing is parallel
    b. Compound pricing is only available if the parent agreement uses a price discount
    c. Compound pricing allows sub agreements to take advantage of discounts specified in parent agreements
    d. The sub agreement discount is calculated first and the resulting price is used to calculate the discount from the parent agreement.

    Answer: c, d

    Explanation:

    Compound Pricing

    In addition to spend accumulation, contract hierarchies include settings that effect the pricing of items.

    Compound pricing allows sub agreements to take advantage of discounts specified in parent agreements. This means that an item covered in a sub agreement may have multiple discounts applied from higher levels in the hierarchy.

    The calculation for compound pricing is serial. The sub agreement discount is calculated first and the resulting price is used to calculate the discount from the parent agreement.

    Compound pricing is only available if the parent agreement uses a percentage discount.

Compound Pricing

- Allows subagreements to take advantage of applicable discounts in parent agreements

- Calculation is serial:
  - Subagreement price discount calculated first
  - Result is then used to calculate parent agreement price discount

72. **Which of the following statement(s) is/are true regarding Override Pricing?**

    Please choose the correct answer.

    a. Requires that parent agreement is a release order contract
    b. If the parent agreement is a release order contract, the system will automatically attach the agreement with the lowest item price
    c. Allows sub agreement price to override parent price
    d. Only b and c
    e. All of the above

    Answer: d

    Explanation:

    Override Pricing:

    - Allows sub agreement price to override parent price
    - Requires that parent agreement is a no-release order contract, otherwise contract with lowest price is automatically selected

    Override pricing allows a sub agreement price to override the price specified in a parent agreement. This occurs when both agreements have item level price discounts specified for the same line item and the parent agreement is a no release order contract.

    If the parent agreement is a release order contract, the system will automatically attach the agreement with the lowest item price.

    When an item's price is determined by a combination of a sub agreement and its parent agreement terms, spend will be accumulated against both of the contracts and tracked using item level accumulators

73. **Which of the following statements are true regarding Milestones?**

    Note: There are 2 correct answers to this question.

    a. Milestones cannot be added to all types of contracts
    b. Amounts can only be associated to milestone in a release order contract
    c. Successful completion of a milestone usually results in payment to the supplier
    d. A milestone is a set of conditions or requirements that must be met by a supplier to achieve the terms of a contract.

    Answer: c, d

    Explanation:

    Milestones:

- Set of conditions or requirements that must be met by a supplier to achieve the terms of a contract
- Supported in Supplier, Commodity and Item level contracts

A milestone is a set of conditions or requirements that must be met by a supplier to achieve the terms of a contract.

Successful completion of a milestone usually results in payment to the supplier. The payment may be triggered by a supplier invoice and verified by a specific user if the contract is a no-release order contract.

Milestones can be added to any level or type of contract, but amounts can only be associated to milestone in a no-release order contract.

74. **Which of the following statements are true regarding Milestones in Release Order Contracts?**

    Note: There are 2 correct answers to this question.

    a. Internal milestones have associated limits that indicate payment amounts.
    b. When you include milestones in no-release order contracts, they are treated as internal milestones only.
    c. They are only used for notification and bookkeeping purposes.
    d. They can include a verifier and a setting to determine when the verifier receives notification relative to the milestone completion date

    Answer: c, d

    Explanation:

    Milestones in Release Order Contracts
    - Used as internal milestones
        - Only for notification or bookkeeping purposes
        - You cannot associate any volume to the milestone
    - No limits associated with internal milestones
    - Set verifier and timing of notification
    - Example: You might set a milestone to ensure that a supplier sends in a requisition report

    When you include milestones in release order contracts, they are treated as internal milestones only. This means they are only used for notification and bookkeeping purposes.

    Internal milestones do not have associated limits that indicate payment amounts. They can include a verifier and a setting to determine when the verifier receives notification relative to the milestone completion date.

75. **Which of the following statements are true regarding Milestones with No-Release Order Contracts?**

Please choose the correct answer.

a. The tolerance is the percent above the maximum amount that can be invoiced or received against the milestone item
b. The maximum amount is the total amount that can be invoiced or received against the milestone item
c. They are only used for notification and bookkeeping purposes.
d. Only a and b
e. All of the above

Answer: d

Explanation:

Milestones in Release Order Contracts:

When you include milestones in release order contracts, they are treated as internal milestones only. This means they are only used for notification and bookkeeping purposes.

Internal milestones do not have associated limits that indicate payment amounts. They can include a verifier and a setting to determine when the verifier receives notification relative to the milestone completion date.

Milestones in No Release Order Contracts:

When you include milestones in a contract without release orders, they are more functional. They may include milestone item limits to determine the amount that a supplier is paid for completing the milestone.

The maximum amount is the total amount that can be invoiced or received against the milestone item.

The tolerance is the percent above the maximum amount that can be invoiced or received against the milestone item.

76. **Which of the following statements are true?**

Note: There are 3 correct answers to this question.

a. In a system that does not include workspaces, only a user with edit access can edit a contract request.
b. In an integrated system that includes contract workspaces, you can edit the contract directly
c. To create a release order, a user must first create a requisition.
d. The creator of a contract is automatically given edit access to that contract.
e. A user can create a release order in 3 ways

Answer: a, c, d

Explanation:

Access Control:

Edit Access
In an integrated system that includes contract workspaces, you cannot edit the contract directly. Instead, you must edit the contract workspace. There is an option in the request wizard to specify a list of users to receive notifications when a contract is approaching its limits.

In a system that does not include workspaces, only a user with edit access can edit a contract request. The creator of a contract is automatically given edit access to that contract. Users on the edit access list will receive notifications when the contract is approaching expiration.

Release Access
A user who has release access to a contract can create release orders that release funds against the contract. To create a release order, a user must first create a requisition. A user can create a release order in the following ways:
- **Auto Attach** - when the user selects an item covered by a contract and the system automatically attaches the appropriate contract to the requisition.
- **Manual Selection** - the user selects items directly from the contract. Users must have the *Direct Release Contract* permission to manually select contracts

Access Control Page

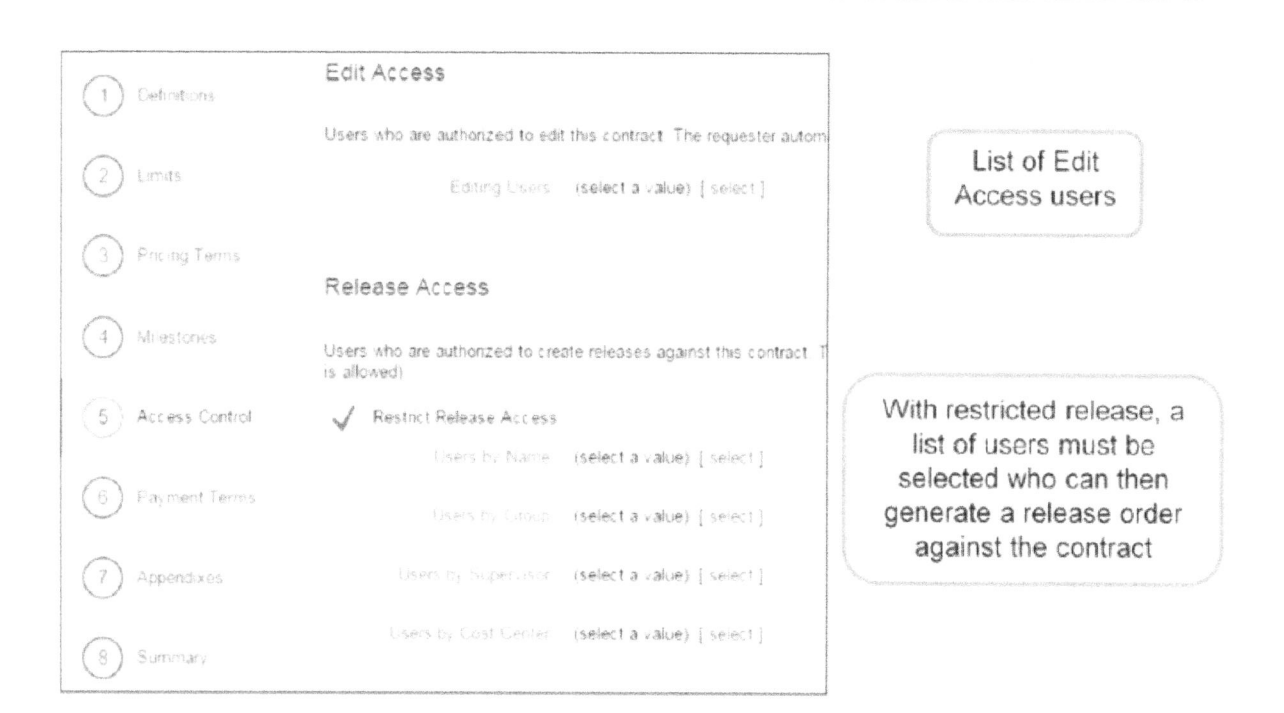

77. **Which of the following statements are true of Appendixes and Attachments?**

Note: There are 3 correct answers to this question.

a. Multiple appendices are not supported
b. Appendixes can be referenced by individual items or the entire contract
c. Attachments are not transmitted to suppliers
d. During a sourcing activity, appendices can be transmitted to suppliers for negotiation
e. An attachment is a document that is considered part of the contract

Answer: b, c, d

Explanation:

Appendices and Attachments
An **appendix** is a document that is considered part of the contract. During a sourcing activity, appendices can be transmitted to suppliers for negotiation.

An **attachment** is a supporting document added as a comment. They are commonly used to justify a request to approvers and are not considered part of the contract. Attachments are not transmitted to suppliers. They are treated as internal documents.

Multiple appendices are supported, such as: terms and conditions, drawings, photos, and so on.

Appendixes can be referenced by individual items or the entire contract.

Appendix
- Document that is part of the contract
- Can be transmitted to suppliers as part of the bid process during a sourcing activity

Attachment
- Supporting document for a contract
- Used to help justify a request to approvers
- Not part of the contract
- They are not transmitted to suppliers

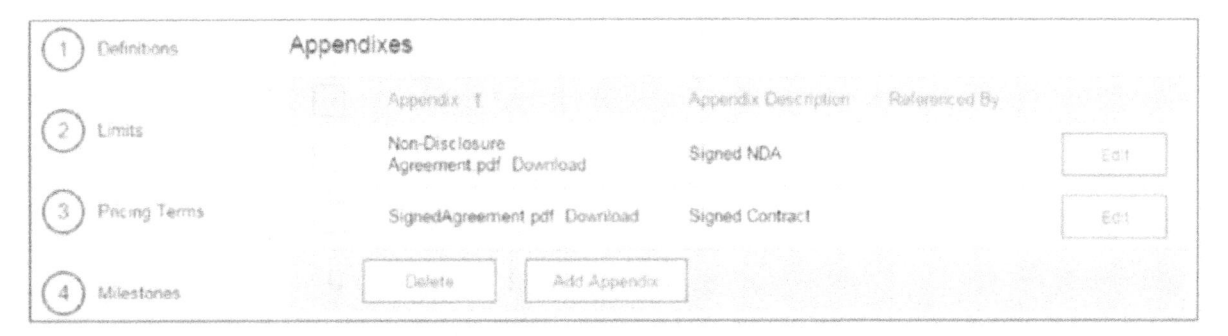

78. **During its creation the contract compliance request (CR) is in which of the following state?**

Please choose the correct answer.

a. Initial
b. Composing
c. Processing
d. Creating

Answer: b

Explanation:

Contract Compliance Request Life Cycle States:

Composing - During its creation the contract compliance request (CR) is in 'Composing' state.

Submitted - Upon submission, the compliance CR is moved into Submitted state. When withdrawn, the request moves back into Composing state.

Approved - A fully approved compliance CR moves into Approved state. If the user has entered a Hold Until date, the compliance CR will stay in the Approved state until the Hold Until date is reached.

Processing - This state immediately follows the Approved state. During the Processing state, the system attempts to create a compliance contract for the contract compliance request.

Processed - After the compliance contract is successfully created, the compliance CR moves into the 'Processed' state.

Contract Request Deleted - While the compliance CR is in Composing or Denied state, the user can decide to delete the request.

Denied - The Denied state occurs when one or more approvers deny approval.

Contract Request Lifecycle

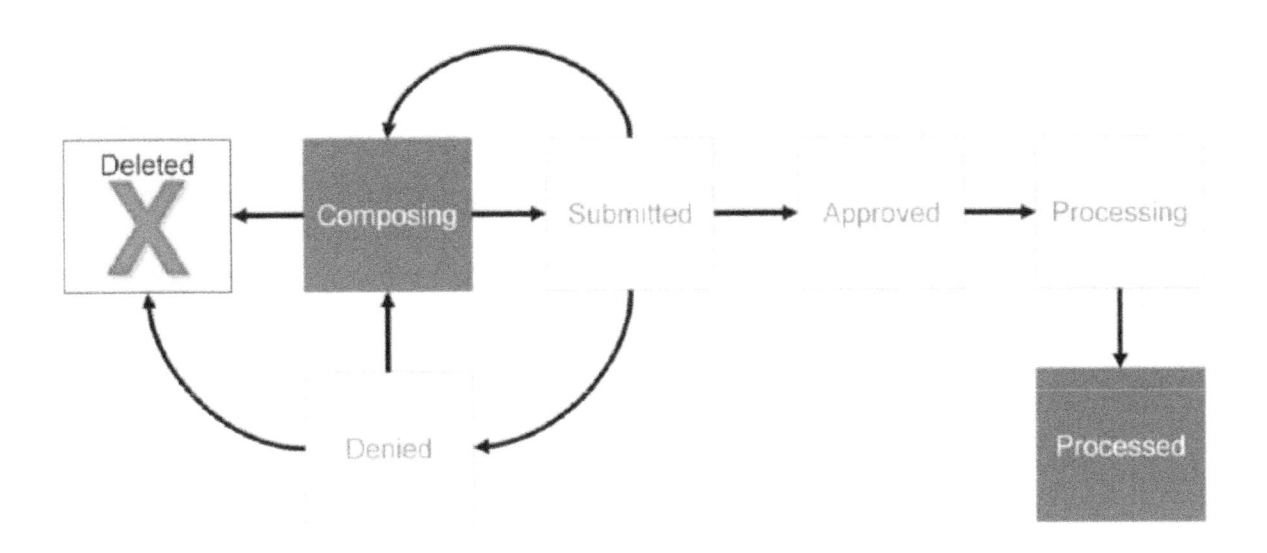

79. **Which of the following statement(s) is/are true regarding Contract Limit Compliance?**

    Please choose the correct answer.

    a. Independent of line-item limits, if the overall limit is exceeded by the specified tolerance, the contract is Closed
    b. The contract is Closed when all item limits exceed tolerances
    c. The contract remains *Open* as long as at least one line-item limit is below tolerance
    d. Only a and b
    e. All of the above

    Answer: e

    Explanation:

    Contract Limit Compliance:

Contract Limit Compliance

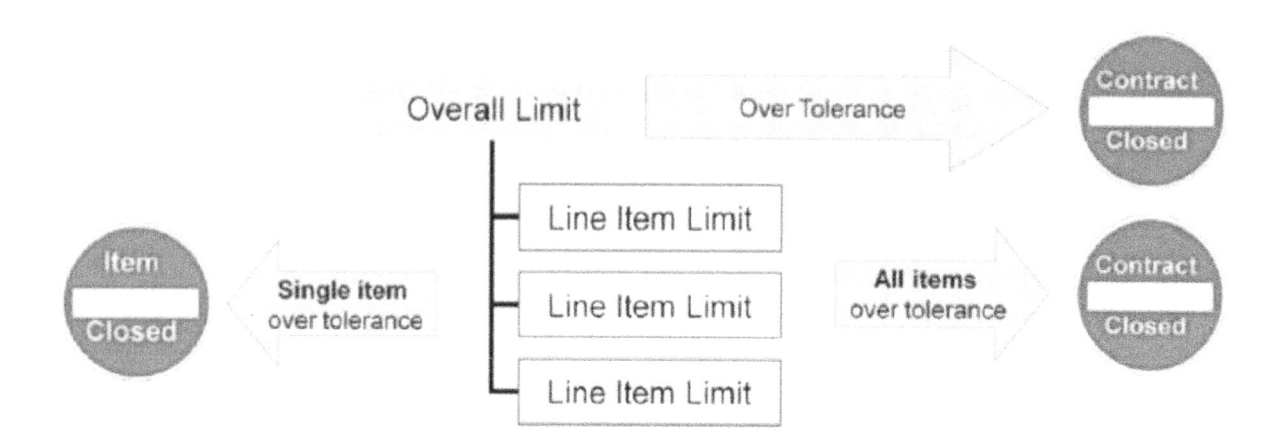

If the contract's limits are exceeded, Ariba will automatically close either the contract or the line items that have exceeded the maximum commitment plus tolerance. This is called "Limit Compliance."

The diagram above illustrates the following compliance rules:

-Overall Limit
Independent of line-item limits, if the overall limit is exceeded by the specified tolerance, the contract is Closed. A contract can go beyond the maximum limit and remain open until the tolerance is reached.

-Line Item Limit
The contract is Closed when all item limits exceed tolerances. The contract remains *Open* as long as at least one line-item limit is below tolerance. Individual items are made unavailable as they exceed their tolerances.

80. **Pricing tiers can be calculated in how many ways?**

    Please choose the correct answer.

    a. 2
    b. 3
    c. 4
    d. 5

    Answer: a

Explanation:

Tiered Pricing

Based on quantity:
- Cumulative or per order
- Used with item-level contracts only
- Available for catalog and non-catalog (contract-based) items

Based on monetary amount:
- Cumulative or per order
- Used with all contract types
- Available for catalog and non-catalog items

Tiered discounts can be defined in one of two ways:
- Based on total **quantity** - only available for item level contracts.
- Based on total **monetary amount** - available with all contract types.

Pricing tiers can be calculated in two ways:
- **Cumulative** - Price breaks are calculated based on cumulative amounts ordered against a contract over time.
- **Per order** - Discount is applied if tier amount or quantity is met on a single order.

81. **Which of the following are features of Ariba Procurement Solution?**

    Note: There are 3 correct answers to this question.

    a. Non Customizable Forms
    b. Built-in reporting
    c. Flexible business rules
    d. Intuitive user interface
    e. High level of security

    Answer: b, c, d

    Explanation:

    Ariba Procurement Solution Features:

    - Intuitive user interface
    - Flexible business rules
    - Enterprise integration
    - Built-in reporting
    - Custom Fields
    - Custom Forms (eForms)

    The Ariba Procurement Solution incorporates major features:

- **Intuitive User Interface** - Employees who have no experience with automated procurement systems can easily use basic functions.
- **Flexible Business Rules** - The Ariba Procurement Solution supports any business process.
- **Enterprise Integration** - Ariba recognizes that the Ariba Procurement System is used in an heterogeneous application environment, where data integration is mandatory.
- **Reporting** - To improve your organization's spend management, you must have visibility into your spend patterns through robust and easy-to-use reporting.
- **Custom Fields** - Your organization can add new fields to the user interface for your specific business needs.
- **eForms** - eForms are custom screens that are designed specifically to support your business processes that are not related to transactional purchasing.

82. **The Ariba Procurement Solution provides choices for integrating with which of the following systems?**

Note: There are 3 correct answers to this question.

a. SAP
b. Oracle
c. PeopleSoft
d. Guidewire
e. Smarter Commerce Suites

Answer: a, b, c

Explanation:

Ariba Procurement Integration

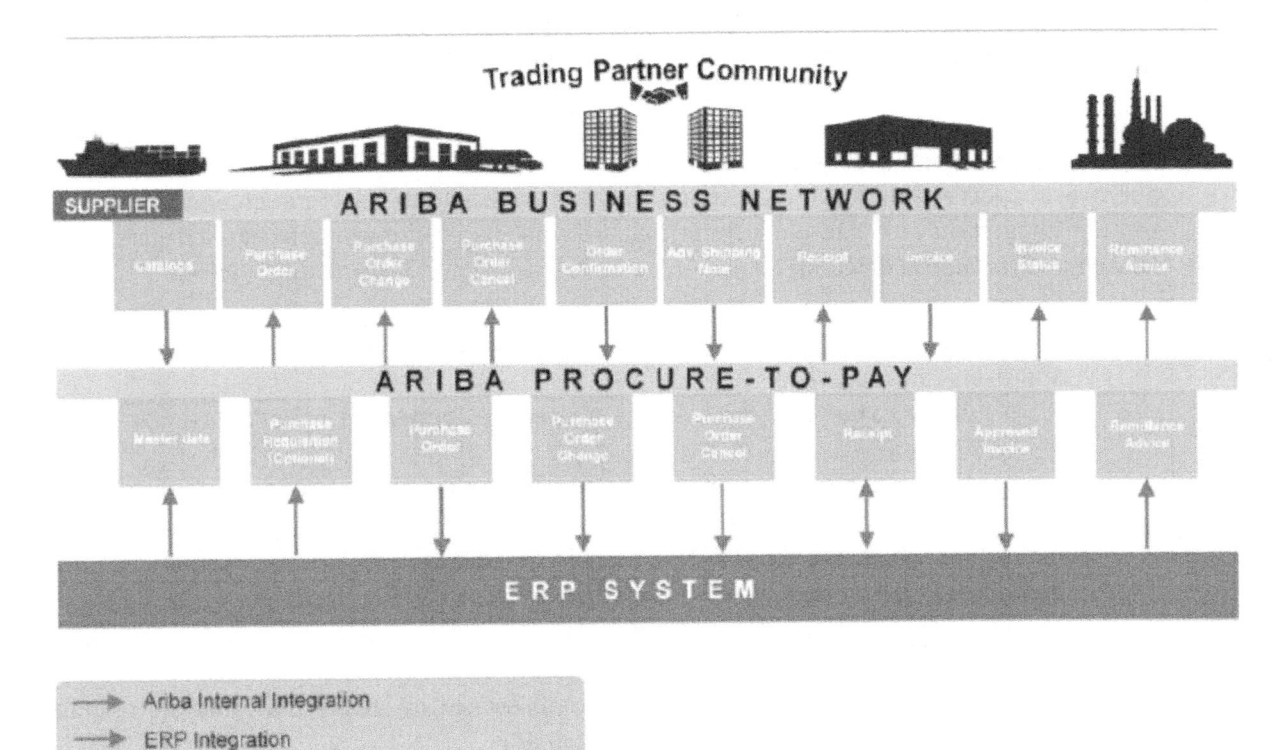

The Ariba Procurement Solution provides choices for integrating with other systems such as SAP, Oracle, PeopleSoft, and other Enterprise Resource Planning (ERP) systems. Enterprise integration is provided by the Ariba Integration Toolkit or other middleware.

83. **Which of the following statements are true regarding Email Approval?**

    Note: There are 3 correct answers to this question.

    a. Email notifications do not contain file attachments
    b. Email approvers can edit approvables
    c. Email approvers can modify approval graphs to add additional approvers
    d. Approver can add comments on the reply email
    e. Approvers can delegate their approval authority for a given approvable by forwarding an email notification

    Answer: a, d, e

    Explanation:

    Email Approval:

The Ariba Procurement Solution generates and sends email notifications to approvers and watchers. Approvers can approve requests by email, without having to open the Ariba Procurement Solution application. Email approval is a powerful feature that supports disconnected approving and delegation of approval authority.

Approvers might often be disconnected from their corporate network and they need a way to approve conveniently even if they are connected to the Internet only intermittently. Email approval support enables customers to perform approvals and denials through email as well as through integration with external systems that are email based (for example, email pagers, web-based email, or mobile devices).

- Approvers receive an email notifying them of a request that requires their approval
- Approvers can approve by:
    - Clicking a button in the message to open the approvable in the Ariba Procurement Solution
    - Clicking the Approve or Deny button in the message to act on the approvable (if HTML email format is enabled)
    - Replying to the email (if text email format is enabled)
- Approver can add comments on the reply email
- Approvers can delegate their approval authority for a given approvable by forwarding an email notification
    - This can be turned off by your administrator to ensure that only the original approvers can take action on a document

Email Approval Limitations:

An approval notification cannot contain file attachments. To view an attachment submitted with an approvable, you must open the approvable document in the Ariba Procurement Solution.

When approving by email, the approver cannot edit an approvable. To edit an approvable, the approver must open it in the Ariba Procurement Solution.

The email approval feature does not allow users to add or delete approvers, or to change approvers in the approval graph. You must use the Ariba Procurement Solution to change the approval graph.

- No file attachments
    - Email notifications do not contain file attachments. Users cannot view attachments before approving
- No editing of approvables
    - Email approvers cannot edit approvables
- No adding or removing approvers
    - Email approvers cannot modify approval graphs to add additional approvers

84. **Which of the following statement(s) is/are true?**

Please choose the correct answer.

a. Users must change/cancel orders in ERP
b. If order was originally sent to ERP, change/ cancel orders can be configured to be exported to the ERP
c. Change/cancel orders are exported to ERP when integration event runs
d. Only b and c
e. All of the above

Answer: d

Explanation:

Export to ERP for Change/Cancel Orders:

- If order was originally sent to ERP, change/ cancel orders can be configured to be exported to the ERP
- Change/cancel orders are exported to ERP when integration event runs
- Users must change/cancel orders in the Ariba Procurement Solution, not in the ERP.

If the original PO was routed through the Ariba Network, the Ariba Procurement Solution handles change or cancel order by sending a new version of the order (a changed or canceled one) to the same supplier. However, if the order is an ERP order, the details of the change and cancel order can be configured to be exported to the ERP system.

Users must initiate change and cancel orders in the Ariba Procurement Solution, not in the ERP.

The process flow is:
- After the changed or cancelled requisition is approved, a new PO version is generated, and the Ariba Procurement Solution exports the changed or canceled PO to the ERP.
- The Ariba Procurement Solution changes the PO status to Ordered (for change orders) or Canceled (for cancel orders).

85. **OK2Pay Files are exported as a zip file which contains which of the following files?**

    Note: There are 3 correct answers to this question.

    a. PaymentHeaderExport.csv
    b. PaymentLineItemDet.csv
    c. PaymentDetailDet.csv
    d. PaymentTaxDetail.csv
    e. PaymentTaxExport.csv

    Answer: a, b, e

    Explanation:

    OK2Pay Files:

- Once invoices are fully reconciled, they can be exported for payment
- Exported as a zip file which contains 5 files:
  - PaymentHeaderExport.csv
  - PaymentLineItemDet.csv
  - PaymentAccountDet.csv
  - PaymentDetailExport.csv
  - PaymentTaxExport.csv
- Export payment info based on date range
- By default it exports all payment info since last export
  - Export can be created manually through UI (Data Import/Export task "Export Payment Requests")
  - Export can be created through Data Transfer Tool, part of the Ariba Integration Toolkit

OK2Pay and Remittance Process

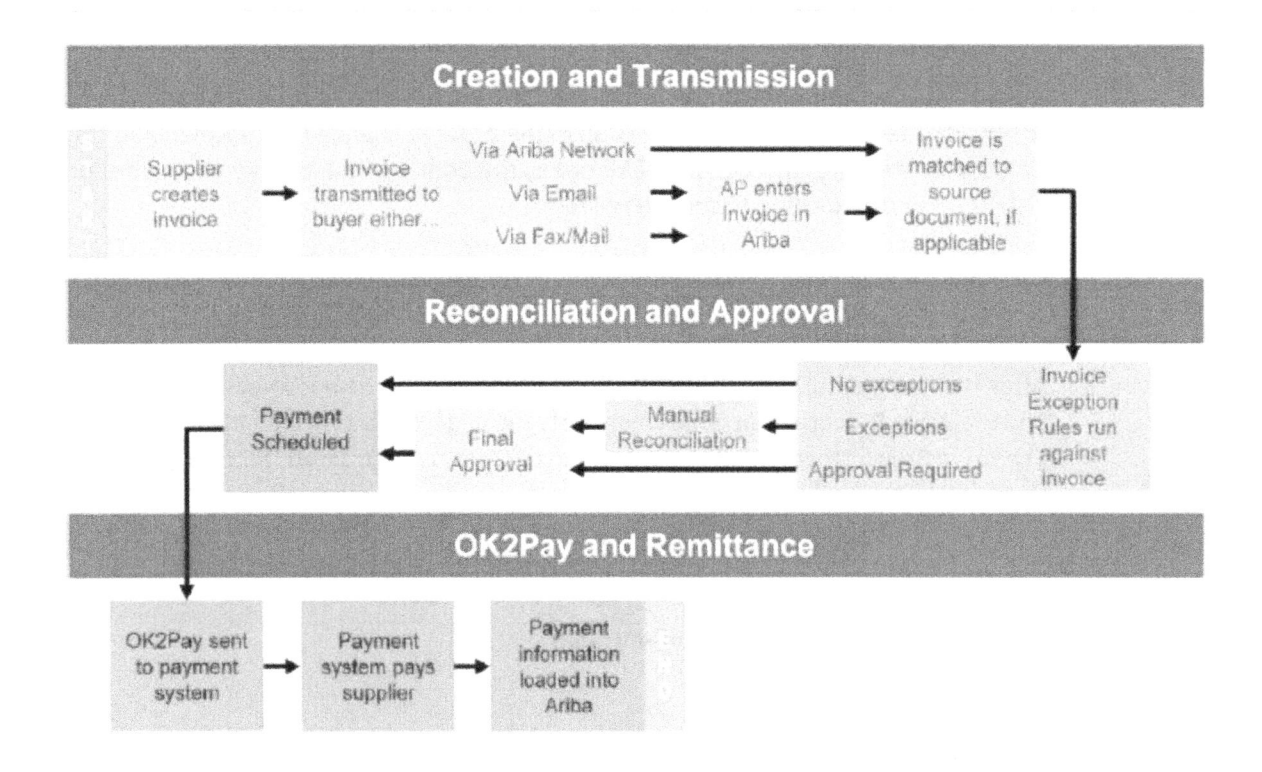

86. **In Receive Export to ERP, which of the following is the source of truth for receipts?**

    Please choose the correct answer.

    a. ERP
    b. The Ariba Procurement Solution
    c. Either a or b
    d. None of the above

Answer: b

Explanation:

Receipt Import from ERP - Receipts can be imported from an ERP system. You import them if receiving is done in the ERP instead of in the Ariba Procurement Solution. Your organization might import receipts if, for example, your ERP system captures inventory tracking information for goods and it is the "source of truth" for this information. Those receipts can then be exported to the Ariba Procurement Solution for use during the PO matching and invoice reconciliation settlement process.

Receipt Export to ERP - Receipts can be exported to an ERP system. You export them if they are generated by the Ariba Procurement Solution, but certain receipt information, such as asset data, must be used by an external asset tracking or inventory management system. Receipt Export is often performed in conjunction with PO export.

Receipt Import/Export can be performed in batch mode through csv flat file integration or "near real-time" through Web Services integration.

Additional Receiving Features

- Asset Data Capture
    - Records asset numbers or locations
- Receipt Import from ERP
    - ERP is the source of truth for receipts
- Receipt Export to ERP
    - The Ariba Procurement Solution is the source of truth for receipts

Ariba Process Knowledge

87. **Withdrawing Requisition puts the request in which of the following status?**

    Please choose the correct answer.

    a. Submitted
    b. Ordering
    c. Denied
    d. Composing

    Answer: d

    Explanation:

    Editing and Withdrawing Requisitions:

Editing:
- Withdraws the request from the approval process
- Puts the request in Composing state and into edit mode
- Allows you to add items, delete items, or change any requisition field

Withdrawing:
- Removes the request from approval process
- Puts the request in Composing status
- Additional step to edit request

Requisition Statuses

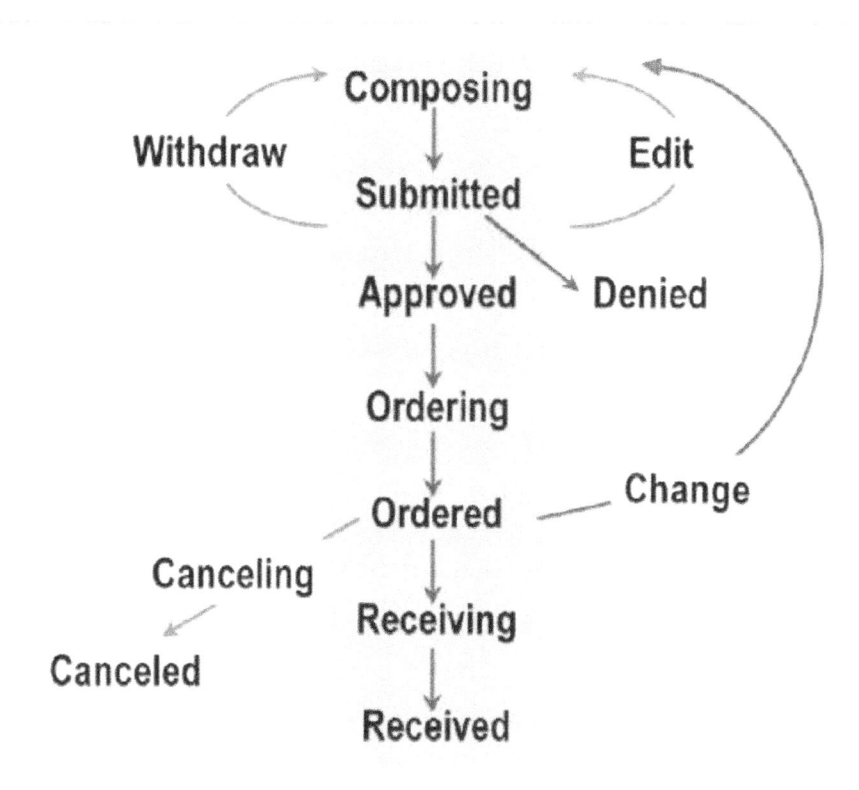

```
         Composing
Withdraw    ↓         Edit
         Submitted
            ↓
         Approved  →  Denied
            ↓
         Ordering
            ↓
         Ordered  ── Change
            ↓
Canceling   ↓
   ↙     Receiving
Canceled    ↓
         Received
```

88. **Which of the following statement(s) is/are true regarding Budget Check Function?**

    Please choose the correct answer.

    a. Budget checking is standard functionality and is enabled by default
    b. Budgets are checked during requisitioning and invoicing
    c. Both a and b
    d. None of the above

    Answer: d

    Explanation:

Budget Check Function:

- Budgets are checked during requisitioning only
- The system checks for adequate funding
- Approval flow based on budget check configuration (or prevent submission of requisitions altogether)
- Budget checking is standard functionality but not enabled by default

Budgets are checked during requisitioning only; they are not checked during invoicing. If your organization receives non-PO invoices or charges for tax, shipping, or special handling on invoices and you want them to apply against a budget, those charges must be entered through a budget adjustment.

If your organization uses budget checking, then every requisition must be associated with a budget, unless a system parameter (Application.Budget.FailCheckOnNoBudget) is turned off. Turning off this parameter results in checking only requisitions that specify a budget.

If budget checking is enabled, a new tab named "Budgets" appears in each purchase requisition. This tab display the budget amount that the requisition consumes, the remaining budget amount, and the time period during which the budget is active.

Your organization has the option to either prevent requisitions from being submitted when budget check fails or allow them to be submitted and then route them for special approval.

89. **By default, a budget is configured to have a threshold percentage of which of the following?**

    Please choose the correct answer.

    a. 60%
    b. 70%
    c. 80%
    d. 90%

    Answer: c

    Explanation:

    Budget Check Exceptions
    The diagram shows the exception scenarios, the outcome, and the user experience. When the budget check function adds the Budget Approver to the workflow, it is more of a warning than a condition of failure. The Budget Approver takes the appropriate action such as assigning a budget or skipping the budget check.

    Thresholds and Tolerances
    Another typical scenario is when the budget check is successful, but results in a warning when the amount exceeds the total available amount or the requisition amount exceeds the associated

budget threshold. By default, a budget is configured to have a threshold percentage of 80%. For example, if a requisition for $80 matches a budget with $100 remaining, a warning message is displayed, although the budget check is successful.

Budget tolerance is calculated and applied on a budget's total allocated amount. For example, assume that a budget period has an allocated amount of $1,000 and a tolerance of 10%, and that a requisition consumes $800 of that budget. The tolerance is not calculated on the remaining amount in the budget, but on the originally allocated amount of $1,000. So when a user creates another requisition for the same budget code, the amount available for consumption is $300 (the remaining $200 plus 10% of $1,000).

90. **Which of the following statement(s) is/are true regarding Accounting – Line Items?**

    Please choose the correct answer.

    a. Each requisition line cannot have a different set of accounting
    b. Accounting can be changed as needed during the transaction flow
    c. Both a and b
    d. None of the above

    Answer: b

    Explanation:

    Accounting-Concepts:
    Accounting fields are used for many business purposes. They are usually used by the general ledger in your ERP system.

    - Accounting fields specify the organizational and financial entities that are affected by a transaction.
    - Called "accounting strings" or "chart fields" in ERP systems
    - Examples of Accounting Fields:
        - Companies
        - Business Units
        - Cost Centers
        - Departments
        - GL Accounts
        - Project Codes
        - Product Codes
        - Regions

    Accounting-Line Items
    Accounting in the Ariba Procurement System is extremely flexible. You can use accounting fields to record departments, cost centers, accounts, projects, or any category supported by your general ledger or ERP systems.

    - Accounting is assigned at the line-item level

- Each requisition line can have a different set of accounting
- The accounting assigned on a requisition remains on that transaction as it flows through system
    - Requisition -> Purchase Order -> Invoice -> Payment Request
    - Accounting can be changed as needed during the transaction flow

91. **You can split accounting for a line item. You might split accounting in which of the following case(s)?**

    Please choose the correct answer.

    a. You might split accounting if an item will be used by multiple departments
    b. You might split if an item must be charged against multiple ledger accounts
    c. Both a and b
    d. None of the above

    Answer: c

    Explanation:

    Split Accounting:
    You can split accounting for a line item. You might split accounting if an item will be used by multiple departments. Or, you might split if an item must be charged against multiple ledger accounts.

    For example, if you are purchasing equipment that will be used by your Marketing, Human Resources, and Finance departments, you would split the accounting three ways and specify the cost centers of those three departments.

    - You can split a line-item's accounting for allocation across multiple entities
        - Split it across multiple Cost Centers, Accounts, Projects, or Departments
        - Impacts the budget of each specified entity
    - Specify a percentage of the line-item amount for each accounting field
        - For example: 60% Marketing and 40% Legal
        - Must total to 100%

92. **Which of the following statements are true regarding Accounting Design?**

    Please choose the correct answer.

    a. Your organization need to use all available accounting fields
    b. Data values for accounting fields are loaded from the ERP
    c. To fill out accounting fields, users select from lists of preloaded values
    d. Only b and c
    e. All of the above

Answer: d

Explanation:

Accounting Design
Your ERP is the source of truth regarding accounting field names and allowed values. The Ariba Procurement Solution loads these names and values and then allows users to select them when specifying accounting in requisitions.

- Your organization does not need to use all available accounting fields
    - Use the ones that are used by your ERP systems
- Data values for accounting fields are loaded from the ERP, which is the "source of truth"
- To fill out accounting fields, users select from lists of these preloaded values

Defaulting
- Users do not have to fill out all accounting fields
    - Some or all of the field values can be defaulted
    - Users can change field values from these defaults
- Defaulting can be based on the commodity:
    - Example: Office supplies are always charged to Account 101325
- Defaulting can be based on the user:
    - Example: Alice belongs to Cost Center 16004

User Default
- show online user profile
- defaults loaded with user master data in User.csv

Commodity Default
- show Partitioned Commodity Code Map online
- default accounting loaded in ERPCommodityCodeMap.csv

93. **Which of the following statements are true regarding Accounting Functionality?**

    Note: There are 2 correct answers to this question.

    a. Accounting cannot determine approval workflows
    b. Accounting can define budgets by only Project Codes
    c. Accounting can drive journal entries in the ERP
    d. Accounting can drive ledger entries in the ERP

    Answer: c, d

    Explanation:

    Accounting Validation:

Accounting Combinations tends to be one of the most complex, voluminous, and difficult files to prepare. It does not exist as a simple extract from the ERP system. Instead, it must be logically constructed using data for individual accounting fields and logic that determines which values for one field are valid in combination with which values for another field.

- Accounting data is loaded from the ERP, which ensures that values are valid in that system
- The accounting values on a transaction are also checked against one another to ensure they are valid in combination
    - PeopleSoft and Generic variants use an Accounting Combination file that specifies valid combinations of values
    - SAP variant uses a collection of combination files that validate pairs of fields

Accounting Functionality:

Accounting affects approvals, budgets, and payment transactions passed back to ERPs.

Accounting can:
- Determine approval workflows
    - Signing-level authority based on Cost Center and Amount
- Define budgets
    - Budgets defined by Project Codes and Accounts
- Drive journal/ledger entries in the ERP
    - Accounting is passed to the ERP on transactions approved for payment

94. **Which of the following statements are true regarding Approval Process Management?**

   Note: There are 3 correct answers to this question.

   a. The Manage Approval Processes page allows your administrator to search for, view, edit, create, and copy approval processes
   b. Each approval process applies to one type of approvable
   c. The administrator can define more than one approval process for each approvable type
   d. More than one approval process can be active for each approvable type at a time.
   e. The administrator cannot manually deactivate an approval process

   Answer: a, b, c

   Explanation:

   Approval Process Management

Approval Process Management

Your administrator builds and manages approval rules using the Approval Processes page in the Manage menu

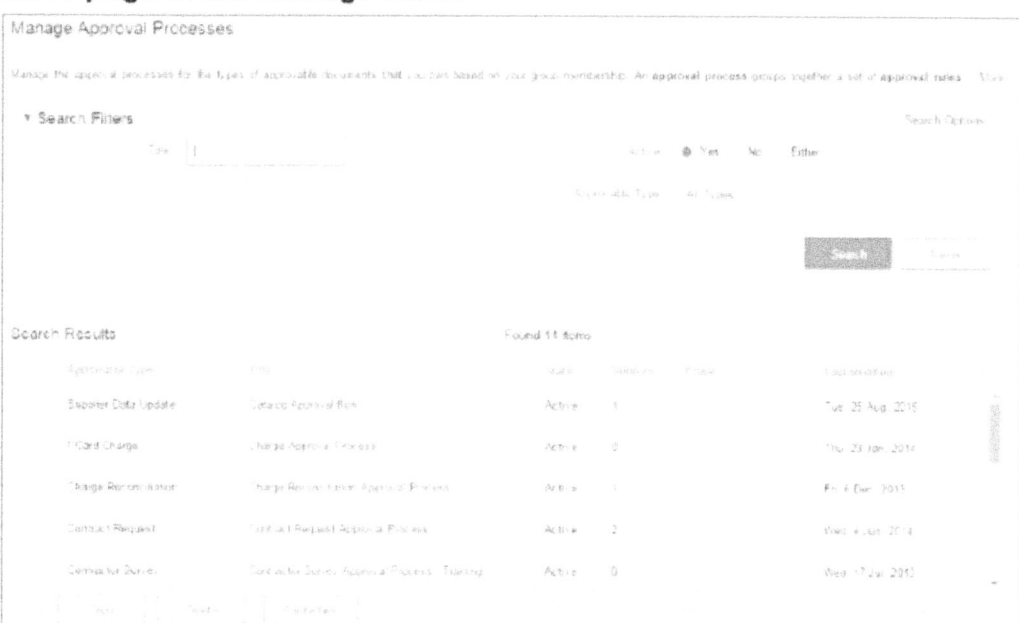

The Manage Approval Processes page allows your administrator to search for, view, edit, create, copy, and delete approval processes. Note that each approval process applies to one type of approvable. The administrator can define more than one approval process for each approvable type, but only one approval process can be active for each approvable type at a time.

After the administrator activates a checked in version of an approval process, the previously active process is deactivated automatically and is added to the history. The administrator can also manually deactivate an approval process or revert to any version for which the **Copy** button is available.

95. **Which of the following statements are true regarding a Purchase Requisition (PR)?**

    Note: There are 2 correct answers to this question.

    a. Legal document, created by the system
    b. Represents a request for products or services from one or more suppliers
    c. Cannot be edited directly
    d. After approval, used to generate one or more purchase orders

    Answer: b, d

    Explanation:

Requisition vs. Purchase Order

A purchase requisition is a document internal to the buying organization that requests goods or services. Typically, it includes internal accounting data (for example, the cost center to be billed) as well as the information needed to generate a purchase order. It might contain requests for goods or services from several suppliers.

A purchase order is a proposed agreement made by the buying organization to one supplier for goods or services. Purchase orders do not usually include internal accounting information that is not relevant to suppliers (for example, GL account codes), but they might include information that is not on requisitions (for example, Terms and Conditions text). It is a proposed agreement, because the supplier has the option to refuse it if the terms, line items, or prices are not acceptable. But, if accepted by the supplier, it becomes a legally binding agreement (that is, a contract) for the supply of the goods or services listed within it.

Requisition vs. Purchase Order

Purchase Requisition (PR)
- Approvable document, created by a user
- Represents a request for products or services from one or more suppliers
- After approval, used to generate one or more purchase orders
- Can be edited to create change orders or cancel orders

Purchase Order (PO)
- Legal document, created by the system and never edited directly
- Represents a proposed agreement (contract) for the supply of goods or services
- Sent to one supplier

96. **The Ariba Procurement Solution supports which of the following order routing methods?**

    Note: There are 3 correct answers to this question.

    a. Ordering through the Ariba Network (AN)
    b. Import to ERP
    c. Manual order
    d. AN order or Manual order with copy to ERP (cc:)

e. Export to CSV

Answer: a, c, d

Explanation:

The Ariba Procurement Solution offers a variety of channels for sending purchase orders to suppliers. In a typical configuration the system supports several alternatives, depending on your ERP systems, your suppliers, and the kinds of items users are ordering.

The Ariba Procurement Solution supports the following order routing methods:
- Ordering through the Ariba Network (AN)
- Export to ERP - The ERP is responsible for sending orders to suppliers
- Manual order - for suppliers that are not on the Ariba Network or in the ERP
- AN order or Manual order with copy to ERP (cc:)

Order Routing Methods

- Transmit Order through the Ariba Network
- Export Order to ERP
    - PO is transmitted to ERP, which then dispatches it to the supplier
- Copy Order to ERP
    - PO is transmitted to supplier via the Ariba Network and a copy is also sent to the ERP
- Dispatch Order Manually
    - PO is manually sent to the supplier (typically by clicking Print on the PO, saving as PDF, and emailing) and the user marks the PO as "Ordered"
- Combinations of the above

97. **Which of the following statements are true regarding PO Quick Enablement?**

Note: There are 3 correct answers to this question.

a. There is no limit to the number and monetary value of the orders that can be transmitted to a supplier during the Quick Enablement process
b. When the Ariba Network routes a PO to a supplier for Quick Enablement, the PO includes an invitation for the supplier to log into the Ariba Network and complete the registration process
c. If you use Quick Enablement, the Ariba Procurement Solution can send purchase orders to suppliers that do not yet have Ariba Network accounts
d. "Manual" suppliers can be enabled to become members of the Ariba Network
e. Ariba Network does not encourage suppliers to take ownership of their accounts

Answer: b, c, d

Explanation:

PO Quick Enablement:

- "Manual" suppliers can be enabled to become members of the Ariba Network.
- PO can be sent to the supplier by fax or email through a temporary Ariba Network account established for that supplier
- The supplier can then take ownership of the temporary account to become fully Network-enabled

If you use Quick Enablement, the Ariba Procurement Solution can send purchase orders to suppliers that do not yet have Ariba Network accounts. For these suppliers, the Ariba Procurement Solution generates an Ariba Network private ID, which are unique per supplier location.

When the Ariba Network routes a PO to a supplier for Quick Enablement, the PO includes an invitation for the supplier to log into the Ariba Network and complete the registration process. Ariba Network encourages suppliers to take ownership of their accounts, which changes the account from a private account to a regular account.

Note that there is a limit to the number and monetary value of the orders that can be transmitted to a supplier during the Quick Enablement process, after which the supplier must accept ownership of their Ariba Network account or else be reverted to a "manual" supplier for purposes of transacting with you.

98. **Change orders are allowed only under which of the following conditions?**

    Note: There are 2 correct answers to this question.

    a. Change orders are allowed in your Ariba Procurement Solution
    b. The PO has no status
    c. The supplier accepts change orders
    d. Your ERP supports change orders (and ERP is not involved in the ordering process)

    Answer: a, c

    Explanation:

    Change Orders:

    - Corrects or changes an order that has already been sent
    - Modifies the underlying requisition that created the PO
    - Change orders are allowed only if:
        - Change orders are allowed in your Ariba Procurement Solution
        - The PO has a certain status
        - The supplier accepts change orders
        - Your ERP supports change orders (and ERP is involved in the ordering process)
    - Change orders can be done by:

- o The original requester
- o Users in certain purchasing-related groups

A change order is a modification to a purchase order that has been sent to a supplier. Your administrator can allow or disallow change orders.

If your organization allows change orders, you can initiate them two ways:
- Change the requisition by clicking the **Change** button in the Requisition screen. This can be performed by the original requester or by users in specific purchasing-related groups (Purchasing/Procurement Manager and Purchasing/Procurement Agent).
- Change the purchase order by clicking the **Change Order** button on the Order tab of the Requisition screen or the **Change** button on the PO screen. (Only members of the Purchasing/Procurement Manager groups can perform the last action.)

Regardless of the way the change is initiated, when you change an order, you are actually changing the requisition from which the order originated. A new version of the requisition, designated by a version number such as V2, is created and submitted for approval. The changes display on the History tab. The new version of the purchase requisition goes through approval and, after it is fully approved, the Ariba Procurement Solution creates new versions of the associated POs and it sends them to the suppliers.

Your administrator can configure the system to enable automatic approval of changed requisitions.

99. **Cancel orders are allowed only under which of the following conditions?**

    Note: There are 2 correct answers to this question.

    a. PO is in Received status
    b. The supplier accepts cancel orders
    c. Your ERP supports cancel orders (and ERP is involved in the ordering process)
    d. Cancel orders are allowed in your Ariba Procurement Solution

    Answer: b, c

    Explanation:

    Cancel Orders:

    - Cancellation of an order that has already been sent
    - Modifies the underlying requisition that created the PO
        - o Deletes all line items
    - Cancel orders are allowed only if:
        - o PO is in Ordered status
        - o The supplier accepts cancel orders
        - o Your ERP supports cancel orders (and ERP is involved in the ordering process)
    - Change orders can be initiated by:

- The original requester
- Users in certain purchasing-related groups

A cancel order is a request to annul a purchase order that has been sent to a supplier.
You can initiate cancel orders two ways:
- By clicking the **Cancel** button on the Requisition View. This can be performed by the original requester or by users with certain purchasing related groups (Purchasing/Procurement Manager and Purchasing/Procurement Agent).
- By clicking the **Cancel** button on the Order tab of the Requisition screen or the Cancel button on the PO screen. Only members of the Purchasing/Procurement Manager groups can perform this action.

Regardless of the way the cancellation is initiated, when you cancel an order, you are actually changing the requisition from which the order originated. It creates a new version of the PR, designated by a version number such as V2, which has all the line items deleted and submits for approval. The changes are displayed on the History tab. During PR approval, the PO moves to Canceling state. After the PR is fully approved, the PO moves to Canceled state. Then, the order cancelation is communicated to the supplier.

Your administrator can configure the system to enable automatic approval of cancelled requisitions.

Cancel orders for "manual" suppliers who are not Ariba-Network-enabled must be dispatched to the supplier manually, and the "Mark Canceled" process must be used to indicate that the change order has been communicated.

100. **Which of the following statements are true regarding Close Order?**

Note: There are 2 correct answers to this question.

a. Closed POs cannot be reopened
b. POs can be closed for change, receiving, invoicing, or all
c. Only Purchasing Administrators can close POs
d. Can automatically close POs that have had no activity for a period of time

Answer: b, d

Explanation:

Close Order:

- Purchasing Administrators and Purchasing Managers can close POs
- POs can be closed for change, receiving, invoicing, or all
- Can automatically close POs that have had no activity for a period of time
- Closed POs can be reopened

POs can be closed if no further activity is expected for them. A typical situation in which you are required to perform a "Close" order action is when a PO has had no activity for a period of time. Closing them allows the creation of more-accurate PO reports.

Other business cases for using the Close Order action are when you:
- Do not want to continue further receiving for a particular item (but can still process open invoices).
- Want to block items in a purchase order, thereby preventing any further receiving or invoicing against particular items in that purchase order.

(If POs were created by users who have left your organization, use delegation to assign those POs to other users; do not close them and open new ones.)

101. **How many ways exist to close a purchase order?**

Please choose the correct answer.

a. 2
b. 3
c. 4
d. 5

Answer: c

Explanation:

There are four ways to close a purchase order:
- **Close for Change** - the PO cannot be changed further
- **Close for Receiving** - the PO cannot have any further receiving done against it.
- **Close for Invoicing** - there can be no further invoicing against the PO
- **Close All Action** - there can be no change, receiving, or invoicing for the PO
- **Adjust and Close for Receiving** - adjust the order when the amount or quantity received is less or equal to the requisition, then close the order You can reduce the order quantity and amount easily without any further transactions on the purchase order. For example, if a purchase order of quantity 20 is partially received and the receipt is for 12, you can close the purchase order for receiving with adjustments.

Bulk Closure: Purchasing Administrators and Managers can close multiple POs for all actions with one command. These users see a **Close for All Actions** button after they perform a PO search.

Automatic Closure: Your administrator can configure the system to automatically close POs that have had no activity for a specified period of time.

102. **Which of the following statements are true regarding Force Order and Force Cancel?**

Note: There are 2 correct answers to this question.

a. The Force Order and Force Cancel commands can be issued by users in the Purchasing Administrator group only
b. The only orders that you can force order are those with a status of Ordering
c. The only orders and payments you can force cancel are those with a status of Canceling
d. The Force Order and Force Cancel commands retransmit the orders

Answer: b, c

Explanation:

Force Order and Force Cancel:

The Force Order and Force Cancel commands are available for circumstances when purchase orders, change orders, or cancel orders are interrupted and have stalled in the Ariba Procurement Solution or on the Ariba Network. You must first search for the stalled order or payment transaction. You must manually communicate the purchase order, change order, or cancel order to the supplier. The Force Order and Force Cancel commands do not retransmit these orders; they only change their statuses in the Ariba Procurement Solution.

These commands can be issued by users in the Purchasing Manager group only.

The **Force Order** command manually changes the status a purchase order or change order in the Ariba Procurement Solution. The only orders that you can force order are those with a status of Ordering.

The **Force Cancel** command manually changes the status of cancel orders or payment transactions in the Ariba Procurement Solution. This command changes the status of the order or payment transaction from Canceling to Canceled and allows the cancellation process to continue. The only orders and payments you can force cancel are those with a status of Canceling.

103. **The Ariba Network sends how many types of status messages to the Ariba Procurement Solution?**

Please choose the correct answer.

a. 2
b. 3
c. 4
d. 5

Answer: b

Explanation:

Order Fulfillment Status:

After a PO is routed through the Ariba Network, users can view the supplier's current order fulfillment status in the Ariba Procurement Solution. The Ariba Network sends three types of status messages to the Ariba Procurement Solution:

- **Order Status:** On receiving the order, the Ariba Network (or a cXML-enabled or EDI-enabled supplier) sends an order status message, indicating that the order arrived intact.
- **Order Confirmation:** The supplier sends an order confirmation, which indicates that ordered line items are accepted, rejected, or backordered. Whenever there is a change to the quantity accepted, accepted with changes, backordered, rejected, or substituted, the supplier sends another order confirmation message.
- **Ship Notice:** When there is a change to the number of items shipped, the supplier sends a ship notice.

Suppliers can generate these messages automatically in their own systems (through cXML or EDI) or create them manually on the Ariba Network.

Order Status Messages

Message	Use	PO Status
Order Status Updates	Indicates that PO has been received electronically at supplier site	Ordering Ordered
Order Confirmation	Reflects status of PO line items: accepted, accepted with changes, rejected, or back ordered.	Confirming Confirmed
Ship Notice	Reflects shipping status of a PO including delivery date, number of items shipped, and carrier used.	Shipping Shipped

Your administrator can configure the Ariba Network to require suppliers to generate order confirmations or ship notices before they can send invoices.

104. **Which of the following is/are the receiving type(s)?**

    Please choose the correct answer.

a. Manually
b. Auto-Receive
c. No Receipt
d. Only a and b
e. All of the above

Answer: e

Explanation:

Receiving Types:

Receiving Types define how receiving is done:
- **Manually:** Receiving is performed by the requisitioner or other designated user.
- **Auto-Receive:** Receiving is performed automatically by the Ariba Procurement Solution.
- **No Receipt:** No receipt is created.

If an order was auto-received, you can click the **Receiving Manually** button to convert the receiving type to Manual so that you can edit the receipt.

Receiving Process and Requisition Status

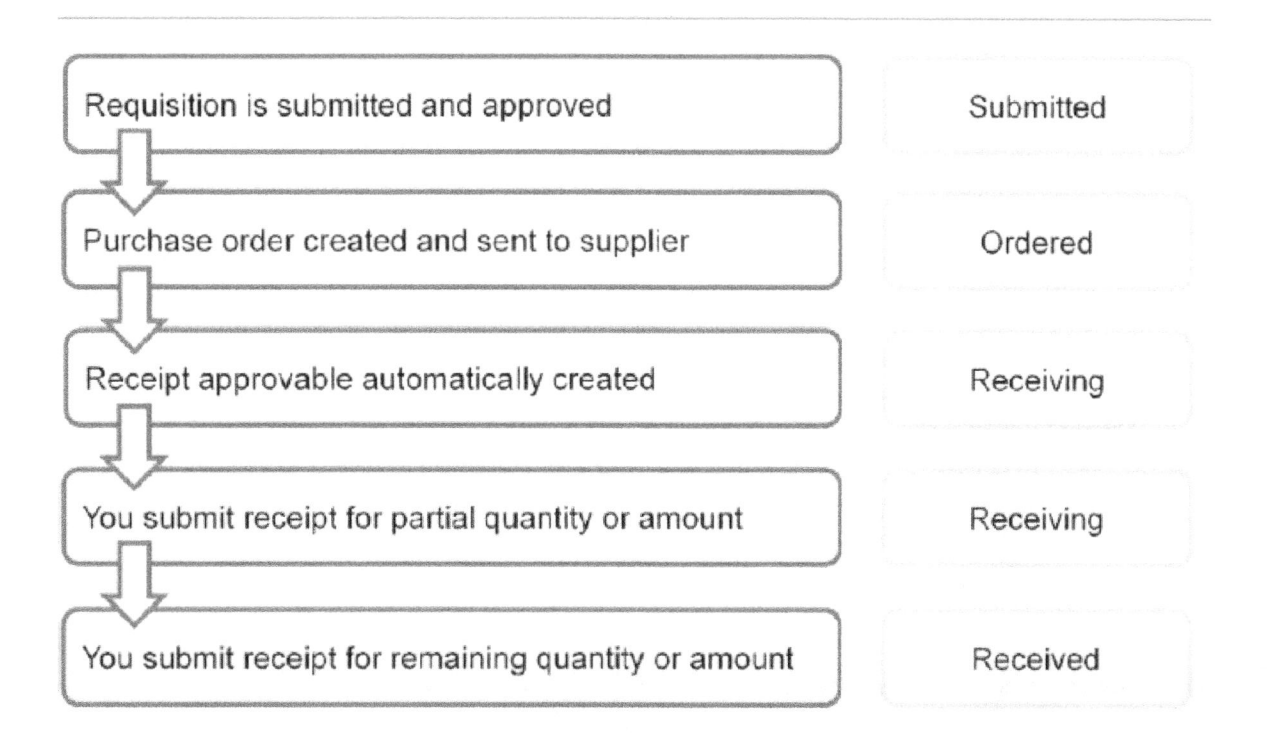

Process Step	Status
Requisition is submitted and approved	Submitted
Purchase order created and sent to supplier	Ordered
Receipt approvable automatically created	Receiving
You submit receipt for partial quantity or amount	Receiving
You submit receipt for remaining quantity or amount	Received

105. **Manual Receipt can be initiated from which of the following?**

Note: There are 3 correct answers to this question.

a. To Do list
b. Receive button on PR/PO
c. Manage → Manual menu
d. Email notification
e. Configure → Manual menu

Answer: a, b, d

Explanation:

Manual Receiving:

Manual receiving steps:
1. Navigate to the purchase order associated with the items you received. The PO must be have status Ordered or Receiving.
2. Edit the receipt (RC) to enter a value for Quantity or Amount.
3. Submit the receipt for approval.

Closing orders - When entering a receipt, you have the option to close the purchase order. You would close the order if you are entering a partial receipt (for less than the full ordered quantity or amount) and do not expect to receive any more against the order. This closes the order for any further receiving.

Rejecting Items - To return products, enter a quantity in the Rejected field. The product return feature creates an audit trail with reasons for the return and the settlement requirements.

Revising Receipts - You can enter a new receipt to revise the quantity or amount for a receipt that has been fully approved. When you create this type of new receipt, you can revise the total received quantity or amount upward or downward (by entering positive or negative values in the Accepted Quantity or Accepted Amount fields). You can enter negative receipts to take corrective action against an order that was previously received (accepted or rejected) with errors. You do this by entering negative amounts

Manual Receipt can be initiated from:
- To Do list
- Receive button on PR/PO
- Manage -> Receive menu
- Email notification

106. **Which of the following is the default receiving type for all receipts?**

Please choose the correct answer.

a. Manual - Receive by quantity
b. Manual - Receive by amount

c. Auto-Receive
d. No Receipt

Answer: a

Explanation:

Default configuration is Manual Receipt, by Quantity

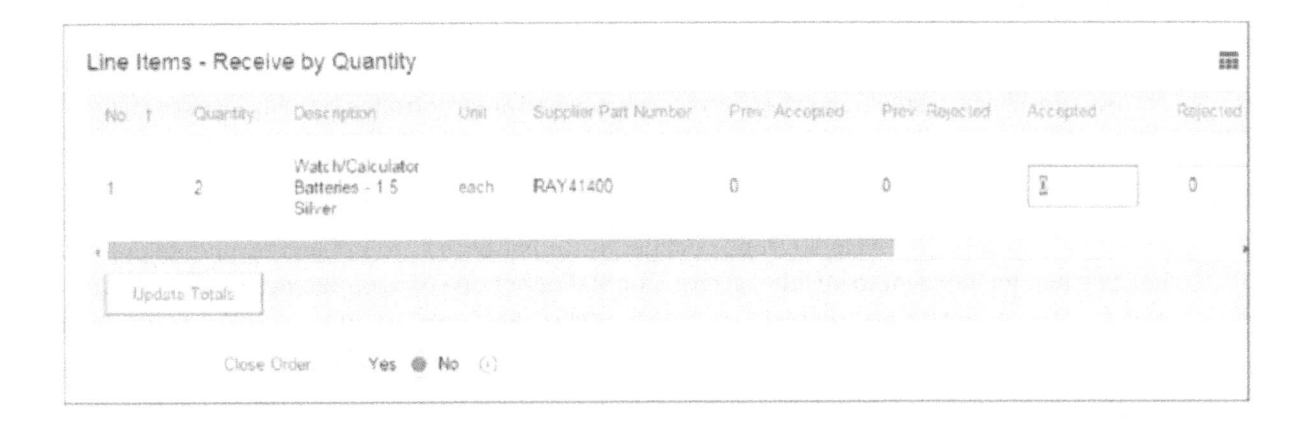

The default receiving type for all receipts is "Manual - Receive by quantity." All orders are received this way unless "auto-receiving" or "receiving not required" is explicitly configured by your administrator.

"Manual - Receive by quantity" means that the receipt information will be manually entered by a user and that user will enter a quantity for each line-item received (instead of entering a monetary amount).

107. **Which of the following statements are true regarding Under-Receiving?**

    Please choose the correct answer.

    a. Allows receipt of a greater quantity or amount than is specified on the PO
    b. Receipts can still be entered for quantities and amounts that are less than under-receiving tolerance
    c. Both a and b
    d. None of the above

    Answer: b

    Explanation:

Over-Receiving
- Allows receipt of a greater quantity or amount than is specified on the PO
- System will not allow entry of quantity or amount that is greater than over-receiving tolerance

Under-Receiving
- Allows POs to be considered fully received, even if quantity or amount received is less than what is specified on PO.
- Receipts can still be entered for quantities and amounts that are less than under-receiving tolerance

Normally, the quantities and amounts on a receipt match the quantities and amounts of the PO. However, you might receive fewer items or for a lesser amount than was specified on the PO (under-receiving), or you might receive more items or for a greater amount than specified on the PO (over-receiving). Under- and over-receiving is allowed and controlled by tolerances configured by your administrator.

Tolerances can be defined based on absolute quantity, percentage of quantity or value, or value (line item amount). The system can be configured so that both absolute and relative tolerances must be met for a receipt to be fully received, or that either one of the tolerance settings must be met for the receipt to be complete. Purchase orders with receipts for which the quantity or amounts are within the tolerance limits are considered fully received and require no further actions.

Most customers allow some level of over-receiving. Over receiving is necessary for some categories - for example, printed materials - where industry best practice is to ship more than the ordered quantity to allow for an expected level of defects.

Most customers do not allow under-receiving tolerances - they set under-receiving tolerance values to zero - because they do not want POs to be considered fully received unless ALL of the ordered quantity has been received.

108. **Which of the following are the invoice efficiency challenges?**

    Note: There are 3 correct answers to this question.

    a. Missed discounts
    b. Inability to forecast cash flow
    c. Invoice disputes and exceptions
    d. Short invoice processing cycles
    e. Short Day Sales Outstanding

    Answer: a, b, c

    Explanation:

Invoicing Process Challenges:

The procurement process can be complex. Every entity participating in procurement is faced with challenges, especially if the processes are not automated.

The Ariba invoicing solutions enable you to electronically automate the invoice matching, reconciliation, exception routing and payment processing activities that traditionally challenge your organization.

Invoicing Efficiency Challenges:

Below given are a number of top invoice efficiency challenges:

- Long invoice processing cycles
- Invoice disputes and exceptions
- Invoice and order line item mismatches
- Late payments
- Duplicate payments
- Missed discounts
- Poor visibility and control over spend
- Inability to forecast cash flow
- Incorrect accounting codes

109. **The Ariba invoicing solutions enable companies to take current invoice management processes and automate which of the following?**

    Note: There are 3 correct answers to this question.

    a. PI2Pay file routing to ERP
    b. Invoice Reconciliation & Exception Handling
    c. Payment status
    d. Reporting
    e. OK2Pay file routing to non-ERP

    Answer: b, c, d

    Explanation:

    Ariba Invoicing Solution:

    The Ariba invoicing solutions enable companies to take current invoice management processes and automate:
    - Invoice Routing
    - Invoice Matching
    - Invoice Reconciliation & Exception Handling

- Invoice Approval Routing Activities
- OK2Pay file routing to ERP
- Payment status
- Reporting

Ariba Invoicing Workflow

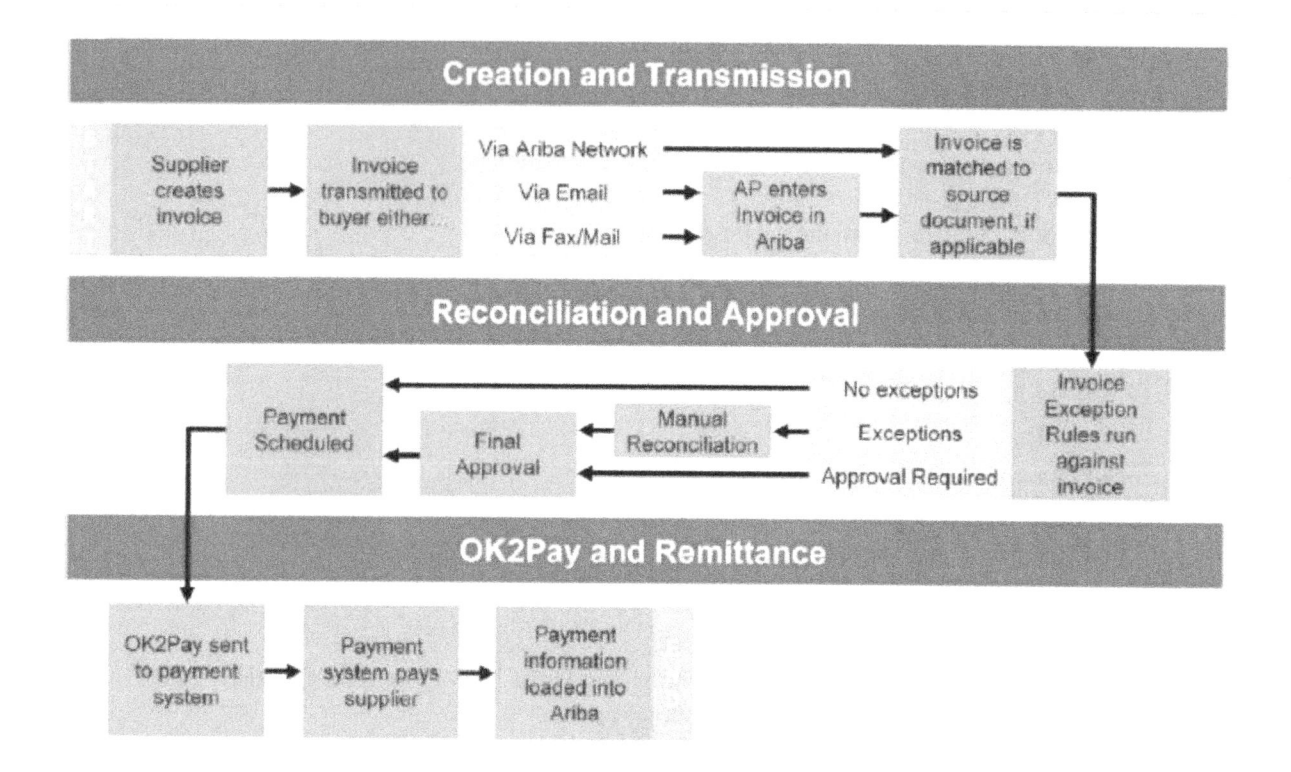

Creation and Transmission

Supplier creates invoice → Invoice transmitted to buyer either... → Via Ariba Network / Via Email / Via Fax/Mail → AP enters Invoice in Ariba → Invoice is matched to source document, if applicable

Reconciliation and Approval

Invoice Exception Rules run against invoice → No exceptions → Payment Scheduled
Exceptions → Manual Reconciliation → Final Approval → Payment Scheduled
Approval Required → Final Approval

OK2Pay and Remittance

OK2Pay sent to payment system → Payment system pays supplier → Payment information loaded into Ariba

110. **There are how many types of invoices in Ariba?**

    Please choose the correct answer.

    a. 2
    b. 3
    c. 4
    d. 5

    Answer: b

    Explanation:

    There are three types of invoices in Ariba:
    - Invoice against a Purchase Order or Release Order - these are called **PO- based Invoices.** PO-based invoices are invoices that are associated with either:
        - a Purchase Order, which was created from a fully approved requisition, and is, essentially, a "standalone" order for goods or services,

- a Release Order, which was created from a fully approved requisition that was itself associated to a release-order contract or a blanket purchase order that requires releases. A Release Order is the mechanism by which funds are released from such a contract/BPO. In Ariba, a Release Order is treated just like a Purchase Order in terms of receiving and invoice reconciliation, which is why invoices against Release Orders are considered to be PO-based Invoices, and not Contract-based Invoices.
- Invoice directly against a Contract or Blanket Purchase Order - these are called **Contract-based Invoices.** Contract-based invoices are invoices that are associated with contracts that were set up to allow direct invoicing, which is typically done for purchases where demand does not need to be communicated to the supplier to prompt the delivery of goods and/or services, and instead the supplier just bills the customer for the goods or services they render. The contract can either be:
    - a No-Release-Order Contract, which is a contract that was set up to **not** require releases and to allow invoicing.
    - a No-Release Blanket Purchase Order (BPO). A BPO is a particular type of contract (not a type of Purchase Order) that is transmitted to the supplier via Ariba Network to facilitate invoicing from AN-enabled suppliers.
- Invoice that is not associated with a Purchase Order, Release Order or a Contract - these are called **Non-PO Invoices.** Non-PO invoices are standalone invoices that are not associated with any other document in Ariba. The term Non-PO can be somewhat misleading, because it makes it sound like it is an invoice that is just not tied to a PO, implying that Contract-based invoices are a type of Non-PO invoice. This is not the case. Non-PO invoices are completely standalone and not tied to a PO/Release Order *or* a Contract/BPO.

Ariba Invoice Types - Ensuring Invoice Compliance

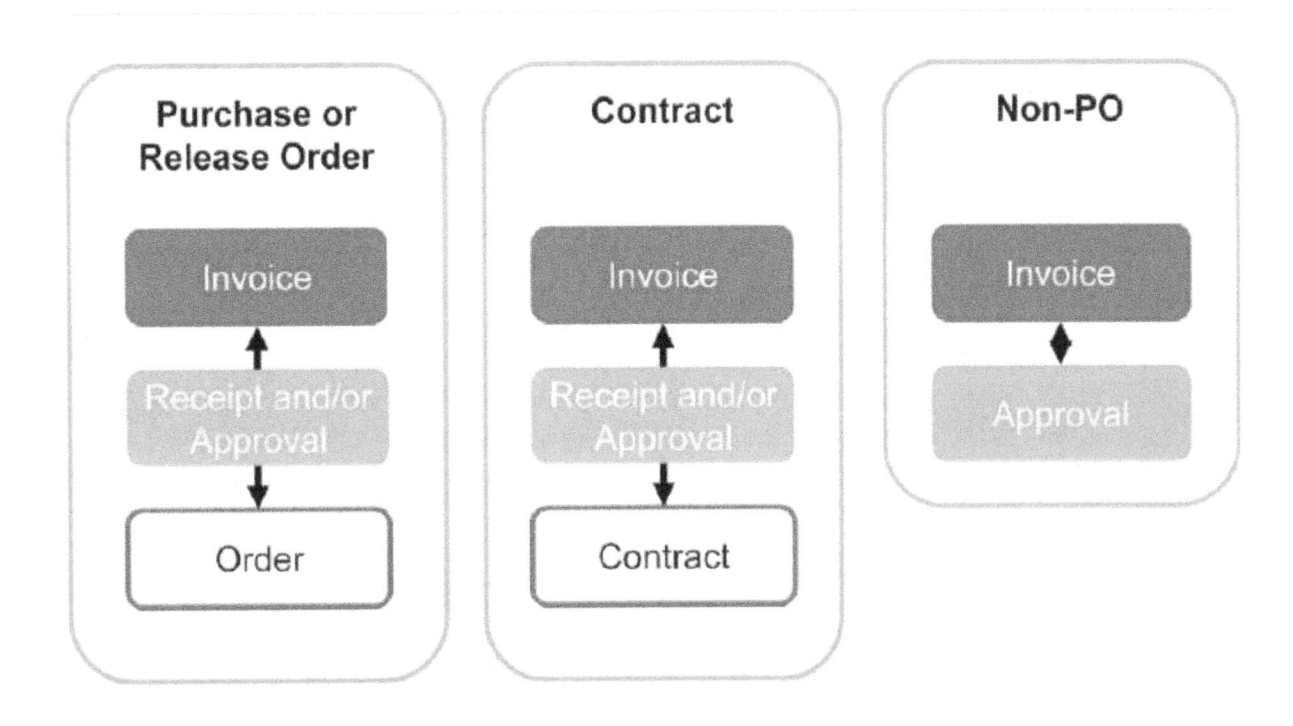

Purchase or Release Order	Contract	Non-PO
Invoice ↕ Receipt and/or Approval ↕ Order	Invoice ↕ Receipt and/or Approval ↕ Contract	Invoice ↕ Approval

111. **Resources that have which of the following groups (permissions) associated with their Ariba user ID can manually enter an invoice?**

    Please choose the correct answer.

    a. Invoice Agent
    b. Invoice Entry User
    c. Invoice Manager
    d. Only b and c
    e. All of the above

    Answer: e

    Explanation:

    Paper Invoicing Methods:

    How will suppliers send you invoices? Does they submit electronic invoices or do they send paper?

    If the supplier sends paper, do they send it to an ICS provider, who converts the invoice into and electronic format and then posts to Ariba Network, or do they send the paper invoice directly to the buyer, who then manually enters the invoice into the Ariba procurement and invoicing solution?

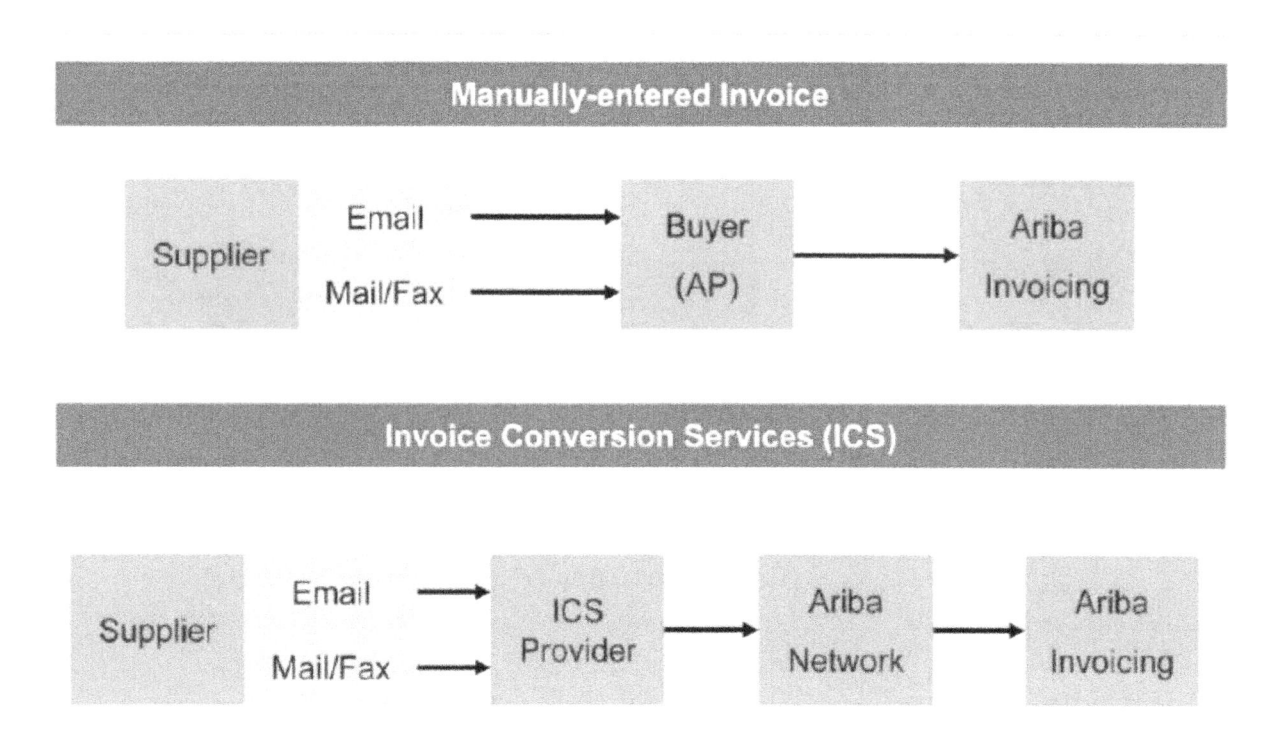

Paper Invoicing Methods

Manually-entered Invoice

Supplier → Email / Mail/Fax → Buyer (AP) → Ariba Invoicing

Invoice Conversion Services (ICS)

Supplier → Email / Mail/Fax → ICS Provider → Ariba Network → Ariba Invoicing

Manually entering invoices:

- If the option to create an invoice is not available, your administrator needs to make a user profile update.
- Resources that have the following groups (permissions) associated with their Ariba user ID can manually enter an invoice:
    - Invoice Agent
    - Invoice Entry User
    - Invoice Manager

Paper Invoice - System User Roles:

An Ariba user who belongs to the Invoice Agent, Invoice Entry User, or Invoice Manager groups logs onto Ariba and creates an invoice from the Create option in either the Command Bar or Common Action panel.

112. **Ariba Network offers suppliers which of the following service that converts a PO into an invoice?**

    Please choose the correct answer.

    a. Contract-based invoicing
    b. PO flip
    c. PO-Invoice
    d. Ariba Network invoices

    Answer: b

    Explanation:

    Supplier Functionality on the Ariba Network:

    PO flip - Ariba Network offers suppliers a service called (manual) PO flip, which converts a PO into an invoice. By inheriting the data from a PO, the supplier can ensure higher accuracy and can auto enforce buyer business rule validation.

    Contract-based invoicing - A supplier creates an invoice against a contract.

    Non-PO invoices - Suppliers can also create a Non-PO invoice without reference to a purchase order. This is useful to suppliers in a number of situations:
    - A supplier wants to create an invoice against an order that was not routed to Ariba Network

    Non -Ariba Network invoices - Suppliers can also post their invoices on Ariba Network using their own invoicing system in the following ways:
    - Over the Internet in cXML format
    - Over Electronic Data Interchange (EDI) networks in ANSI X12 format

Ariba Network Invoice Creation PO Flip Workflow:

If the supplier is Ariba Network enabled, Ariba Network sends the Supplier an email notification each time a PO is submitted.

A background process on Ariba Network downloads and sends a copy of the invoice to your Ariba procurement and invoicing solution.

Process – PO Flip

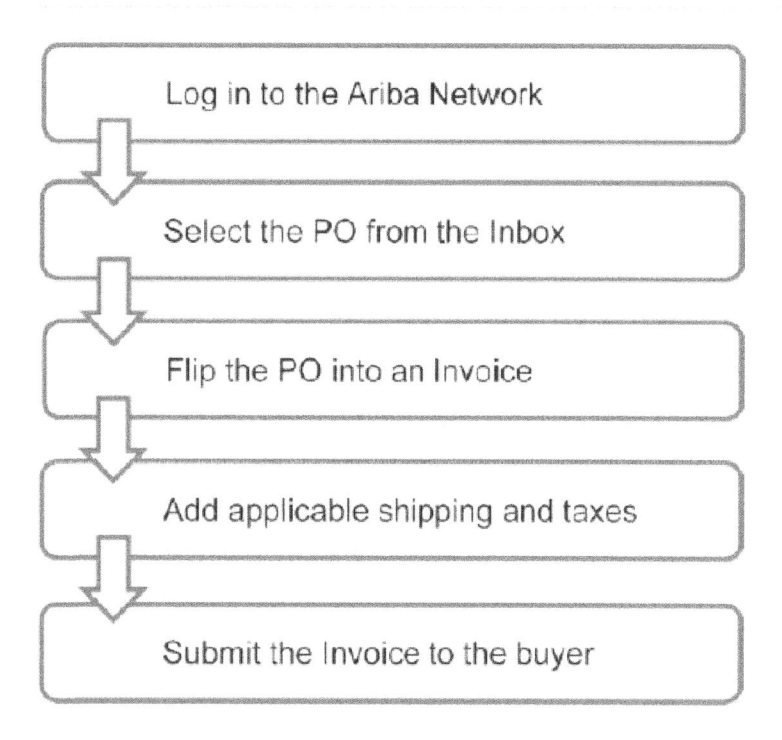

- Log in to the Ariba Network
- Select the PO from the Inbox
- Flip the PO into an Invoice
- Add applicable shipping and taxes
- Submit the Invoice to the buyer

113. **Contract-based invoices can be created and transmitted in which of the following option(s)?**

    Please choose the correct answer.

    a. Electronic invoices
    b. Manual invoices
    c. Both a and b
    d. None of the above

    Answer: c

    Explanation:

Contract-based Invoicing:

Contract-based invoices can be created and transmitted both as electronic invoices and manual invoices.

Contract-Based Invoicing

Creation and Transmission

START → Supplier creates invoice → Invoice transmitted to buyer either... → Via Ariba Network / Via Email / Via Fax/Mail → AP enters invoice in Ariba → Invoice is matched to source document, if applicable

Reconciliation and Approval

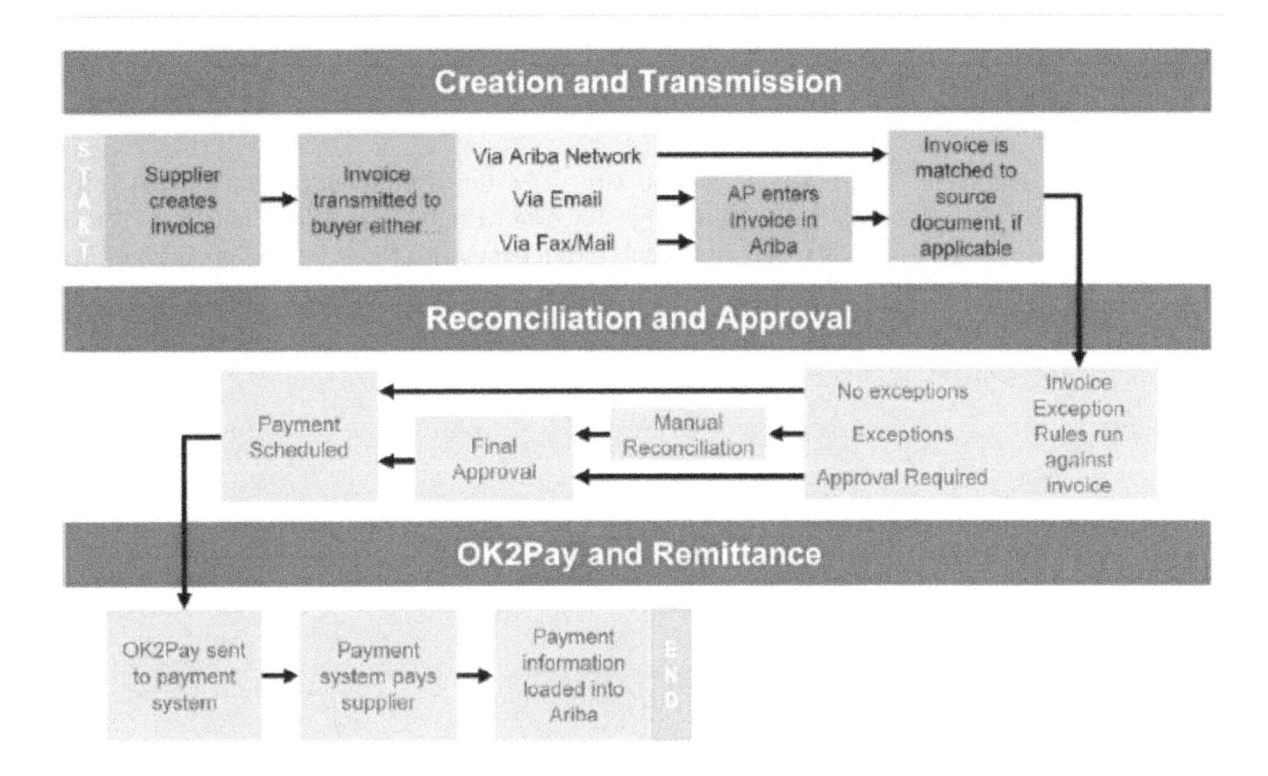

Invoice Exception Rules run against invoice → No exceptions / Exceptions / Approval Required → Manual Reconciliation → Final Approval → Payment Scheduled

OK2Pay and Remittance

OK2Pay sent to payment system → Payment system pays supplier → Payment information loaded into Ariba → END

114. **Which of the following statements are true regarding Contract-based Invoice?**

    Note: There are 2 correct answers to this question.

    a. A contract-based invoice is an invoice aligned with an existing contract or blanket purchase order within Ariba
    b. Suppliers cannot do contract-based invoicing through the Ariba Network.
    c. Contract-based invoicing enforces negotiated contract terms and pricing
    d. A contract-based invoice is an invoice that is entered and matched against a release order contract

    Answer: a, c

    Explanation:

    Contract-based Invoice:

    - **An invoice that is entered and matched against a no-release order contract**

- Enforces negotiated contract terms and pricing
- Contract-based invoice process is aligned with the PO invoice reconciliation process
- **Use Cases**
  - Enforce Contract Pricing on invoices
  - Tiered Pricing Term invoices
  - Fixed and Recurring Payment Term invoices
  - Service Milestone No Release Order (No 30) Invoicing
  - Reseller Pricing Terms

A contract-based invoice is an invoice aligned with an existing contract or blanket purchase order within Ariba. Instead of matching the incoming invoice with a PO, Ariba will match the invoice against the contract terms. Suppliers can do this through the Ariba Network. This process enforces negotiated contract terms and pricing.

Contract-based Invoicing

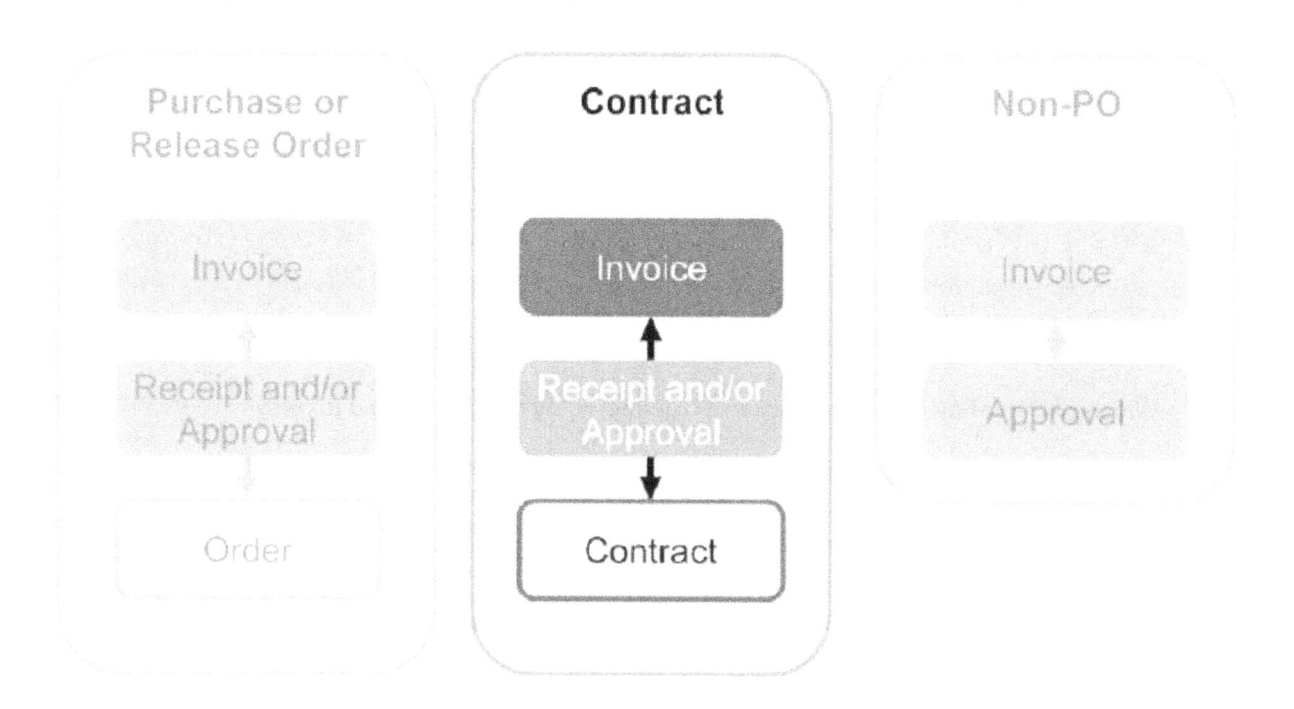

115. **Which of the following invoices have no matching documents?**

   Please choose the correct answer.

   a. Contract-based Invoices
   b. PO-based Invoices
   c. Non-PO Invoices

d. Non-Contract Invoices

Answer: c

Explanation:

Invoice Types:

Non-PO invoices have no matching documents. Instead of matching to an Order or Contract and Receipt, there will typically be an approval process.

By routing the non-PO invoice to an approver, we can ensure the invoice is accurate and can be paid.

Non-PO Invoicing

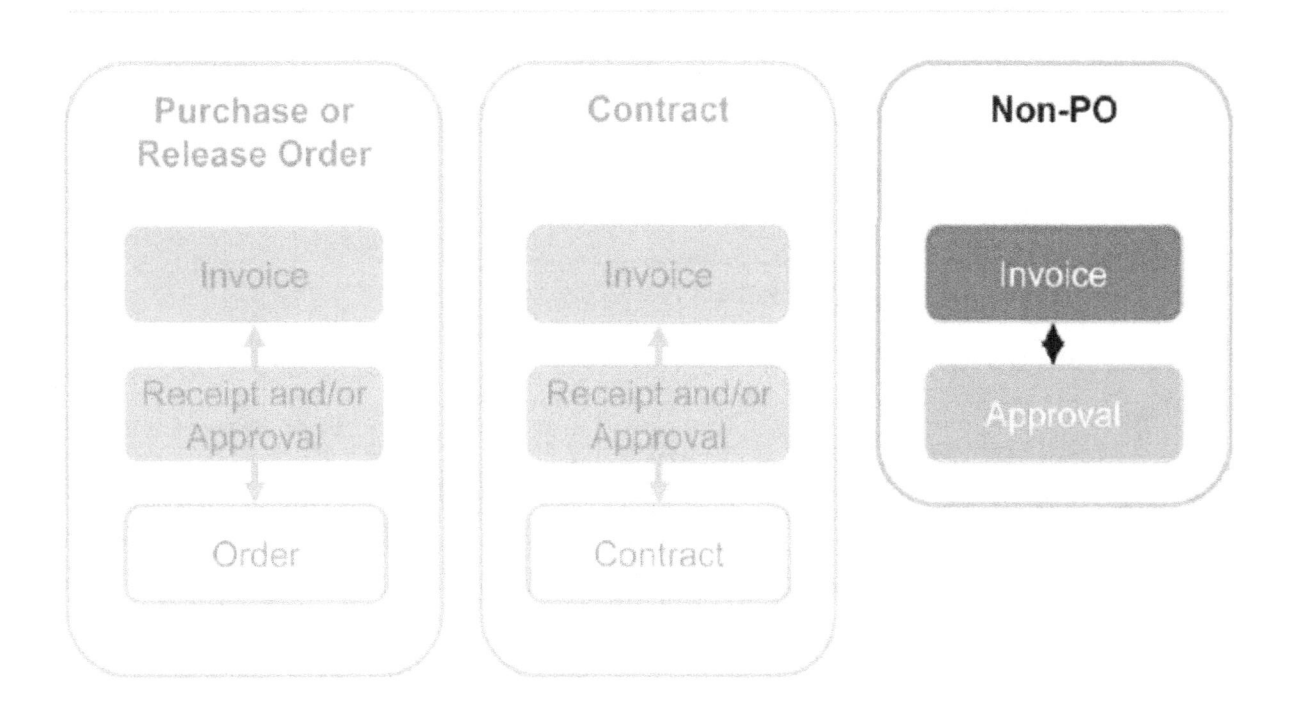

116. **Which of the following are use cases for Non-PO Invoices?**

    Note: There are 2 correct answers to this question.

    a. Unmanaged spend category
    b. Control over price or quantity of goods or services
    c. Typically will require approval to ensure invoice is accurate and goods/services from the invoice were delivered
    d. Tiered Pricing Term invoices
    e. Reseller Pricing Terms

Answer: a, c

Explanation:

Non-PO Invoice Use Cases:

- Unmanaged spend category
- No control over price or quantity of goods or services
- Typically will require approval to ensure invoice is accurate and goods/services from the invoice were delivered

A Non-PO invoicing is a workable solution for some spend types. If your organization is able to negotiate these same categories of spend in advance, more control will be gained over pricing terms and provide the ability to forecast spend commitments and savings.

Process – Non-PO Invoices on the Network

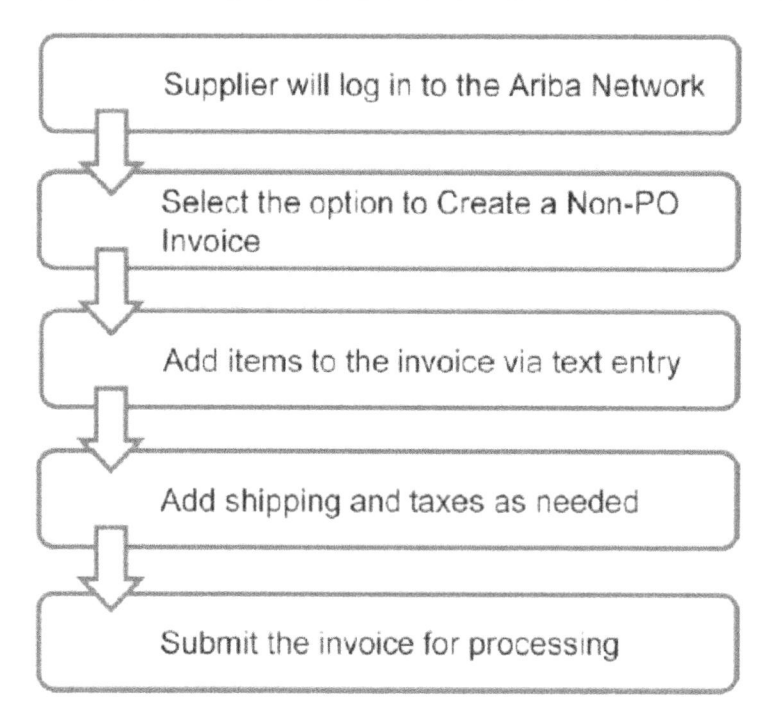

Supplier will log in to the Ariba Network
↓
Select the option to Create a Non-PO Invoice
↓
Add items to the invoice via text entry
↓
Add shipping and taxes as needed
↓
Submit the invoice for processing

117. **Which of the following statements are true regarding a Credit Memo?**

    Note: There are 2 correct answers to this question.

    a. A credit memo must be associated to a cancelled/void payment
    b. A credit memo must be associated to a purchase order
    c. Credit memos are typically entered at the line item level

d. A credit memo is performed so that the invoice accumulation can be adjusted

Answer: c, d

Explanation:

Credit Memo Overview:

A credit memo:
- is a credit or refund from the supplier back to you.
- may or may not be associated to a purchase order.
- is typically entered at the line item level.
- is entered the same way you enter an invoice; except the line item price is negative.
- is performed so that the invoice accumulation can be adjusted.

Credit Memo Use Cases:

Refunds - For example, if your company purchased equipment that was later returned, the supplier might first issue an invoice and then (after the return) a credit memo, which represents the amount due to be refunded to you.

Discounts - Supplier submitted invoice before applying a discount.

Kickback - Supplier returns of a part of a sum received often because of a confidential agreement.

Creating a Credit Memo:

- Credit Memos follow the same process as invoices
- The only major difference is that amounts on a credit memo must be negative
- Use a dash to represent negative numbers, e.g. -100

118. **Which of the following statements are true regarding Invoice Reconciliation (IR)?**

    Note: There are 2 correct answers to this question.

    a. IR contains a record of the reconciliation process.
    b. Invoice Reconciliation numbers does not have same numbering scheme as Invoices
    c. The IR document is generated only when exceptions are not generated
    d. The Invoice Reconciliation (IR) is a copy of the original invoice

    Answer: a, d

    Explanation:

    The two primary documents used in invoicing are:

Invoice (INV)

When an invoice arrives from the Ariba Network, the invoice document never gets touched or modified. You can consider it a master document and for audit reasons must be left the way it arrived.

Invoice Reconciliation (IR)

The Invoice Reconciliation (IR) is a copy of the original invoice. It contains a record of the reconciliation process. This document is used for the reconciliation process instead of the original invoice which is saved as is. The Invoice Reconciliation (IR) indicates the history: an invoice has arrived, been matched to an order, validated, and any exceptions found that were addressed by an invoice exception handler or the requestor. Invoice Reconciliation numbers have the same numbering scheme as Invoices with the prefix of "IR" (e.g. IR1234-152). The IR document is always generated regardless of whether exceptions are generated or not.

Invoice Reconciliation Terminology

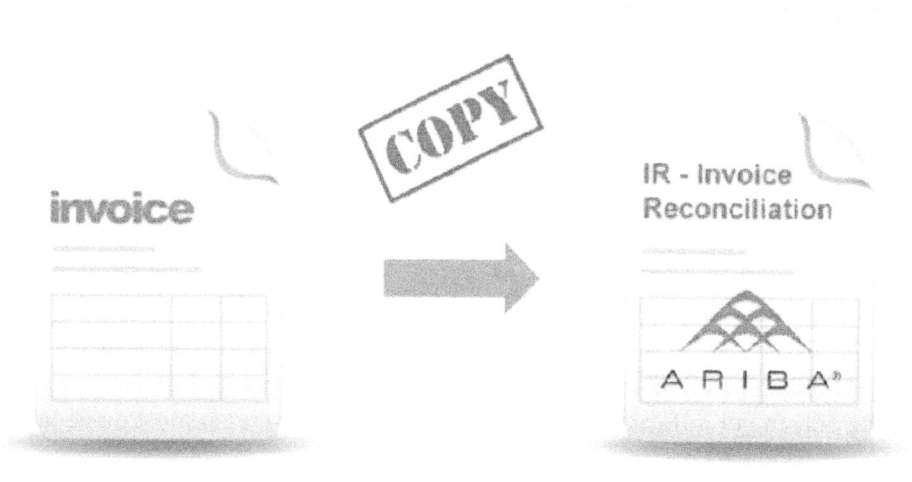

The invoice sent by the supplier.
The contents of this invoice do not change.
All reconciliation will occur using the IR document.

A DUPLICATE of the invoice which is used for processing.
This is where most (or often all) approvals will occur.

119. **In Invoice Validation, Customers need to decide whether to use Header level validation or Line item level validation based on which of the following?**

    Note: There are 3 correct answers to this question.

    a. Commodity type
    b. Cost center
    c. Controlling area
    d. Transaction size
    e. G/L Account

Answer: a, b, d

Explanation:

Invoice Validation:

- Compares the line items and amounts on the invoice to the line items and amounts on the PO in Ariba
- Header Validation compares invoice summary amount to order summary amount and receipt summary amount
- Line-level Validation throws an exception if any line item is out of tolerance

All matched invoices are validated against the criteria configured. The validation is rule based with tolerances and a workflow process for exception handling.

Depending upon the commodity type, transaction size, cost center or receiving practice, customers need to first decide which of the following two methods they will use for validation:

- Header level validation
- Line Item level validation

120. **The invoice reconciliation engine utilizes which of the following tolerance configurations settings for invoices below a configurable threshold?**

    Please choose the correct answer.

    a. Skip
    b. Auto-Accept
    c. Auto-Reject
    d. Only a and b
    e. All of the above

    Answer: e

    Explanation:

    Validation Tolerance Operations:

    The goal of automatic reconciliation is to handle the straightforward cases directly and to refer any outstanding issues to designated exception handlers, who can address those issues manually.

    In the default configuration, the invoice reconciliation engine also looks for invoices that are "easy" to accept or reject and sets those up to require as little manual processing as possible.

    The invoice reconciliation engine utilizes the following tolerance configurations settings for invoices below a configurable threshold:

- Skip
- Auto-Accept
- Auto-Reject

For Ariba Procure-to-Pay and Ariba Invoice Professional, tolerance configurations are set with the associated Invoice Exception type using the Invoice Exception task in the Ariba Administrator dashboard.

121. **Which of the following validation tolerance operation is typically used to reduce the workload for invoices with minor deviations from the PO?**

    Please choose the correct answer.

    a. Skip Amount
    b. Auto Accept Amount
    c. Auto Accept Percentage
    d. Auto Reject Amount
    e. Auto Reject Percentage

    Answer: c

    Explanation:

    Auto Accept Percentage is typically used to reduce the workload for invoices with minor deviations from the PO

Validation Tolerance Operations

Skip Amount
- Validation is skipped when the invoice amount is less than Skip Amount.
- *No exception is created.*
- Typically used to reduce the workload for invoices for low-cost items.
- Default: $5

Auto Accept Amount
- Accepts the invoices when the invoice amount is less than the Auto Accept Amount.
- An exception is created but accepted automatically
- Typically used to reduce the workload for invoices for low-cost items
- Default: $10

Auto Accept Percentage
- Accepts the invoices when the invoice amount is less than a specified percentage of the original order
- An exception is created but accepted automatically
- Typically used to reduce the workload for invoices with minor deviations from the PO
- Default: 0.15 (15%)

122. **Which of the following statements are true regarding Auto Reject Invoice?**

    Note: There are 2 correct answers to this question.

    a. The invoice reconciliation engine cannot choose to automatically reject an invoice
    b. An invoice is rejected automatically if an invoice exception occurs
    c. The automatic reconciliation phase always creates an invoice reconciliation document and submits it for approval, even if the automatic reconciliation process has indicated that the document should be auto-accepted or auto-rejected
    d. The approver cannot see the results of the automatic reconciliation

    Answer: b, c

    Explanation:

    Auto Reject Invoice:

    - Rejects invoices if the automatic validation process could not find a matching order.
    - Creates an invoice reconciliation document and submits it for approval.

The invoice reconciliation engine can choose to automatically reject an invoice. An invoice is rejected automatically if an invoice exception occurs. For example, in the default configuration, the "Invalid Invoice Data" exception causes an invoice to be auto-rejected.

The automatic reconciliation phase always creates an invoice reconciliation document and submits it for approval, even if the automatic reconciliation process has indicated that the document should be auto-accepted or auto-rejected.

The approver can see the results of the automatic reconciliation and can either approve it or continue to make changes. For example, an approver can use the Cancel Reject command to change the auto-reject recommendation, or edit the line items to suggest an alternative reconciliation.

Invoice Validation Examples – $100 Purchase Order

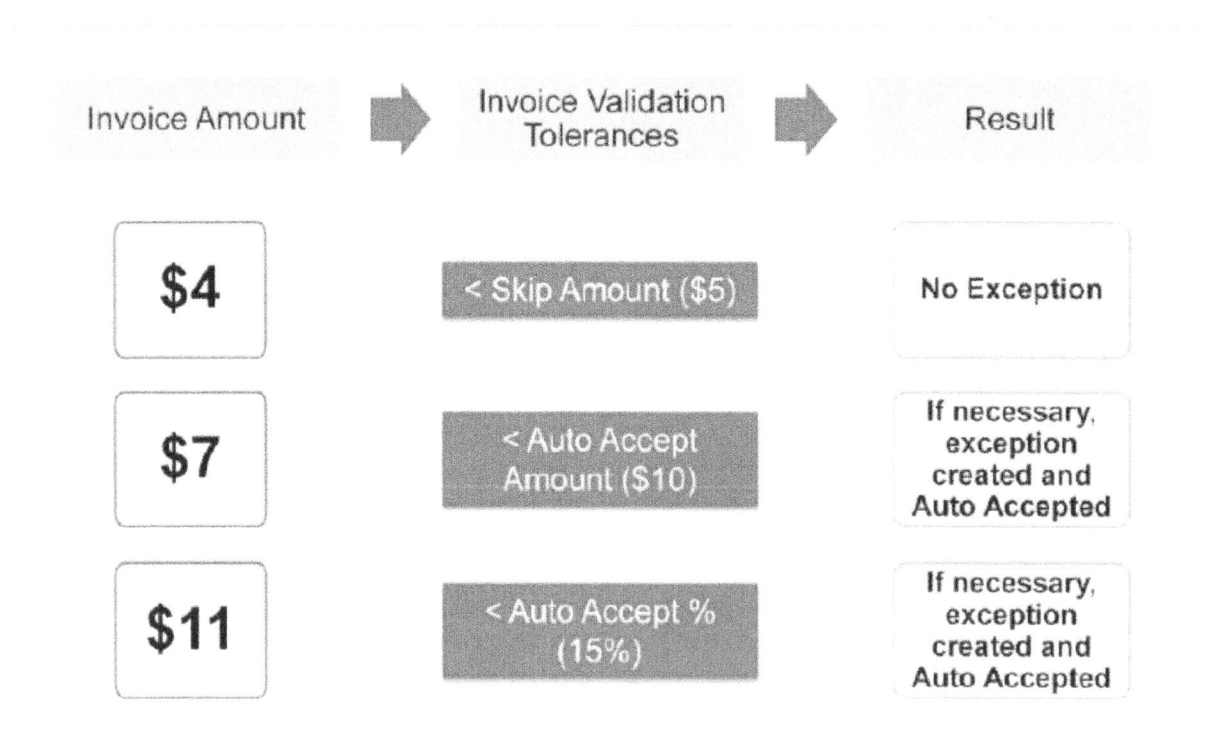

Invoice Amount	Invoice Validation Tolerances	Result
$4	< Skip Amount ($5)	No Exception
$7	< Auto Accept Amount ($10)	If necessary, exception created and Auto Accepted
$11	< Auto Accept % (15%)	If necessary, exception created and Auto Accepted

123. **Which of the following are Invoice Reconciliation – Line Actions?**

    Note: There are 3 correct answers to this question.

    a. Edit
    b. Dispute
    c. Submit
    d. Manual Match
    e. Refer

Answer: a, b, d

Explanation:

Invoice Reconciliation - Line Actions:

Use the **Edit** command to update the IR line item data.

Use the **Accept** command to accept the header exception.

If you **Dispute** the exception, you indicate that the invoice amount or quantity is incorrect. The values on the original purchase order (not the invoiced amount) are marked for payment.

Use the **Manual Match** command only if you want to match the IR to a different purchase order or contract line item other than the one to which it has been automatically matched.

Use the **Cannot Resolve** command to pass on an exception you are not sure how to handle to the next approver(s) in the approval flow. This is not an option for the last person on the approval flow.

Invoice Reconciliation - Header Actions:

When an Invoice Reconciliation (IR) document has the status Reconciling, the exception handler for that document must suggest a recommended action, specifying whether to accept, dispute, or resolve that exception. You can also take additional action, as necessary such as adding comments at the line or header level or clicking Add Attachment to attach a document to the IR document.

The exception handler can take action either at the header level (affecting the entire invoice) or the line item level (affecting only a single exception).

Submit sends the processed reconciliation for further approval.

Reject sends the entire invoice back to the supplier. The supplier is responsible to submit a new, corrected invoice. If you reject an invoice, all invoice exceptions are flagged as Rejected to indicate you have not accepted any exceptions.

Refer is used when you are not sure how to deal with the exception, but you know someone who can. You refer the exception to an individual/role who is not otherwise on the approval flow.

Manual Match is used if the invoice is matched to the wrong purchase order or contract, or if the system could not find a matching order or contract and raised an Unmatched Invoice Exception error.

124. **Which of the following statement(s) is/are true regarding Tax Exceptions?**

    Please choose the correct answer.

a. Tax Exceptions may require additional processing in order to be paid
b. Tax Exceptions can be Accepted or Rejected
c. Both a and b
d. None of the above

Answer: a

Explanation:

Tax Exceptions:

- Tax Exceptions may require additional processing in order to be paid
- Tax Exceptions cannot be Accepted or Rejected
- For example:
    - If a tax rate calculation fails, a Tax Calculation Failed exception is created
    - The tax rate must be adjusted in the tax tables
    - The reconciler will then click the Recalculate Tax button
    - The exception will be cleared if the tax tables now can calculate the correct tax rate

If a Tax Calculation Failed exception has been detected the Recalculate Tax button is displayed. Most likely this indicates that your tax table does not support the configuration of the invoice. For example, you may be shipping to a destination that is not listed in the tax table, and so the comparison of the Ship From and Ship To address to calculate the sales tax fails. To resolve the exception, you must first correct your tax table, and then reconcile the exception by clicking the Recalculate Tax button.

Best Practices

125. **For Supplier Data Management, which of the following is the best practice adoption based on Procurement Cost?**

Please choose the correct answer.

a. Master data is synchronized between various systems (accounting, purchasing, etc.) to prevent data duplication, accurate reporting and to support marketing initiatives
b. Single vendor record per vendor with a formal process/rules for new vendor set up
c. System gives suppliers the ability to maintain their own data and upload their own content to the buyer's catalog and supplier data management repository
d. None of the above

Answer: a

Explanation:

Master data is synchronized between various systems (accounting, purchasing, etc.) to prevent data duplication, accurate reporting and to support marketing initiatives is the best practice for Supplier Data Management based on Procurement Cost.

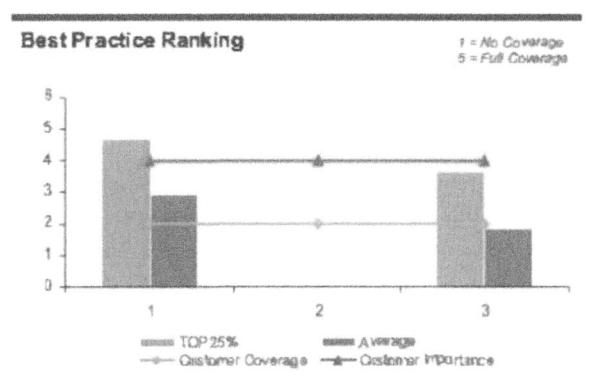

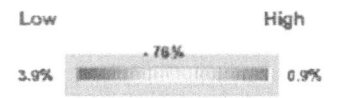

126. **For Supplier Collaboration, which of the following is the best practice adoption based on Procurement Cost?**

    Please choose the correct answer.

    a. Supplier portal supports stock requirements inventory level checks
    b. Suppliers are able to maintain their own data, pre-enter goods receipts (ASNs), and pre-enter invoices on behalf of the buying organizations (approval is required)
    c. Company facilitates order collaboration through a supplier portal for order acknowledgements, advanced shipping notifications, and confirmations
    d. Strategic suppliers are viewed as part of the team and collaborate with engineering as well as sourcing to ensure components and finished products can meet expectations

    Answer: c

Explanation:
Company facilitates order collaboration through a supplier portal for order acknowledgements, advanced shipping notifications, and confirmations is the best practice for Supplier Collaboration based on Procurement Cost.

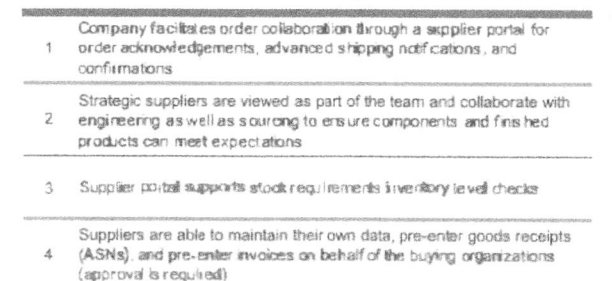

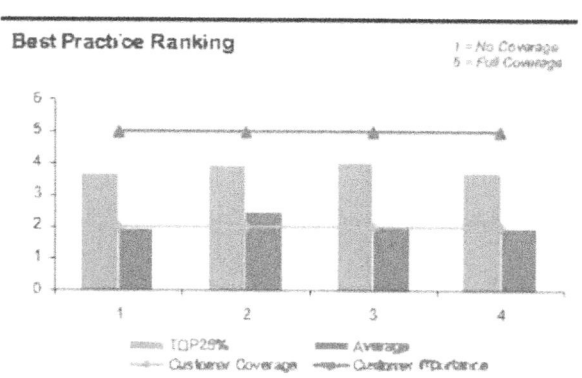

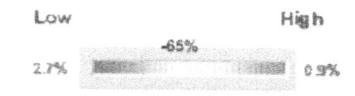

127. For Supplier Enablement, which of the following is the best practice adoption based on FTEs?

    Please choose the correct answer.

    a. Suppliers have capability to self-register via a supplier portal
    b. Purchasers can approve suppliers registering via the supplier portal; once approved, Suppliers can maintain their own administrative information
    c. Supplier portal supports stock requirements inventory level checks
    d. None of the above

    Answer: b

    Explanation:

Purchasers can approve suppliers registering via the supplier portal; once approved, Suppliers can maintain their own administrative information is the best practice for Supplier Enablement based on FTEs.

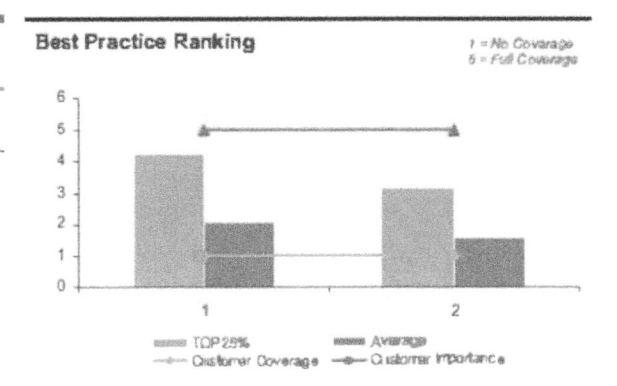

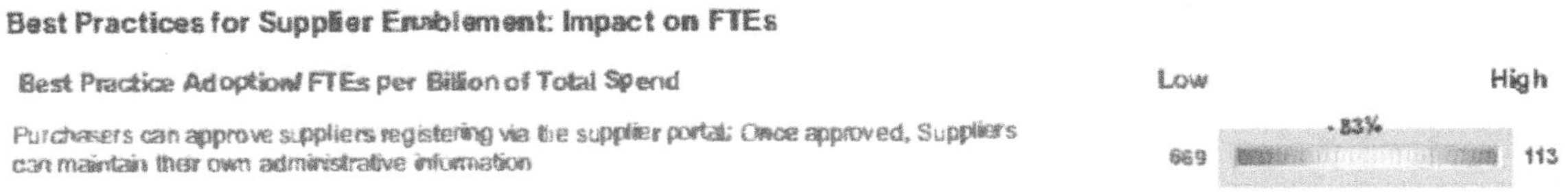

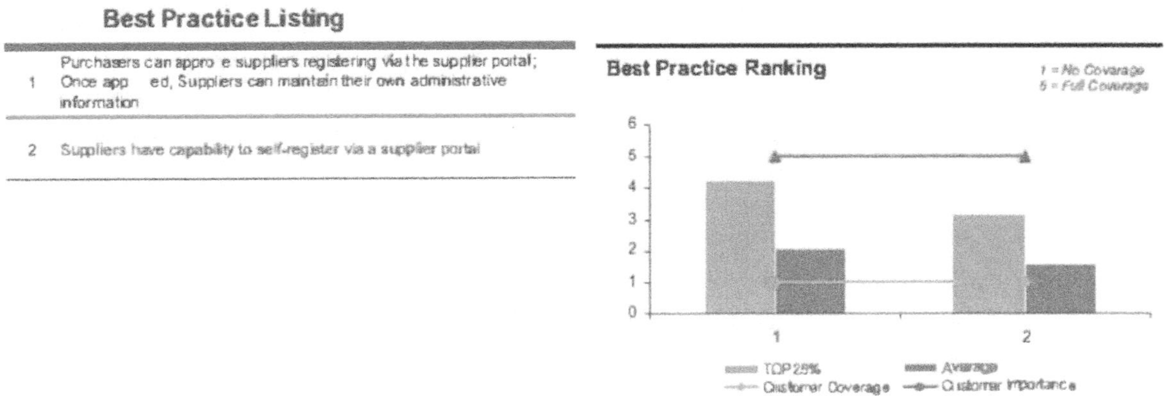

128. **For Supplier Performance Management, which of the following is the best practice adoption based on Average Annual Savings?**

    Please choose the correct answer.

    a. System tracks quantitative (price, delivery) and qualitative (quality, service) KPIs of supplier performance; performance is regularly communicated to supplier
    b. Organization has real-time visibility into supplier performance and related risks for pro-active improvements
    c. Suppliers performances are measured on a regular basis to review if they are meeting contract terms and to gain leverage in negotiation
    d. None of the above

    Answer: a

    Explanation:

Organization has real-time visibility into supplier performance and related risks for pro-active improvements is the best practice for Supplier Performance Management based on Average Annual Savings.

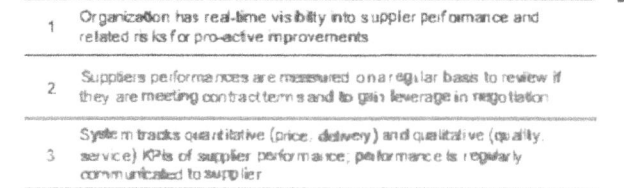

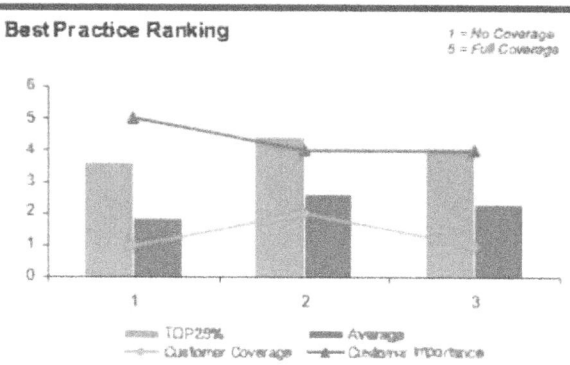

129. **For Sourcing (Category Management), which of the following is the best practice adoption based on Annual Savings?**

    Please choose the correct answer.

    a. Category experts and/or councils strategically manage top spend categories and conduct regular spend reviews to identify new opportunities of contract
    b. Organization fosters supplier competition for commodity spend to further reduce price and achiever true market value
    c. System has ability to aggregate purchases across all business units for accurate global analysis of supplier spend data
    d. None of the above

    Answer: b

    Explanation:

    Organization fosters supplier competition for commodity spend to further reduce price and achiever true market value is the best practice for Sourcing (Category Management) based on Annual Savings.

Best Practice Listing

1	Category experts and/or councils strategically manage top spend categories and conduct regular spend reviews to identify new opportunities of contract
2	Organization fosters supplier competition for commodity spend to further reduce price and achieve true market value
3	System has ability to aggregate purchases across all business units for accurate global analysis of supplier spend data

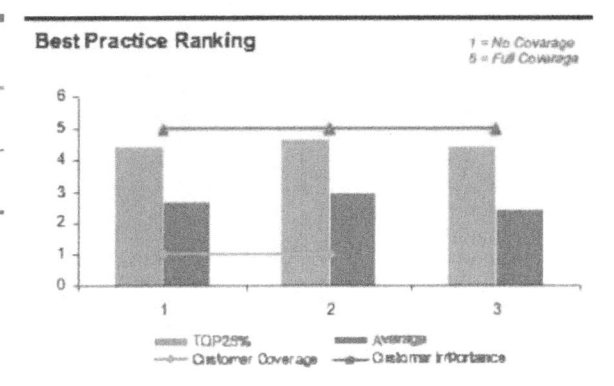

Best Practice Ranking (1 = No Coverage, 5 = Full Coverage)

Best Practices for Sourcing (Category Mgmt.): Impact on Annual Savings and E-Sourcing

Best Practice Adoption/ Average Annual Savings-Direct (in %)	Low		High
Organization fosters supplier competition for commodity spend to further reduce price and achieve true market value	3.7%	+62%	5.9%

Best Practice Adoption/ Spend Sourced Via e-Auctions-Indirect (in %)	Low		High
System has ability to aggregate purchases across all business units for accurate global analysis of supplier spend data	9.7%	+92%	18.6%

130. **For Sourcing (Supplier Evaluation), which of the following is the best practice adoption based on Annual Savings?**

    Please choose the correct answer.

    a. Organization has access/subscription to on-line supplier network with enabled automated customer-supplier matching for new suppliers' discovery and assessment
    b. Organization negotiates and manages contract terms for vendor managed inventory. Automatic replenishment, early-pay/volume discounts for commodities
    c. Formal request for information, proposal, and quotation prices is in place to collect multiple supplier responses for both new and renegotiated buys
    d. Follow formal multi step sourcing process which includes spend analysis, strategy development and execution

    Answer: c

    Explanation:

    Formal request for information, proposal, and quotation prices is in place to collect multiple supplier responses for both new and renegotiated buys is the best practice for Sourcing (Supplier Evaluation) based on Annual Savings.

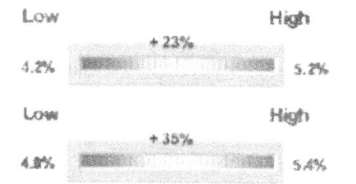

131. **For Compliance, which of the following is the best practice adoption based on Purchase Orders?**

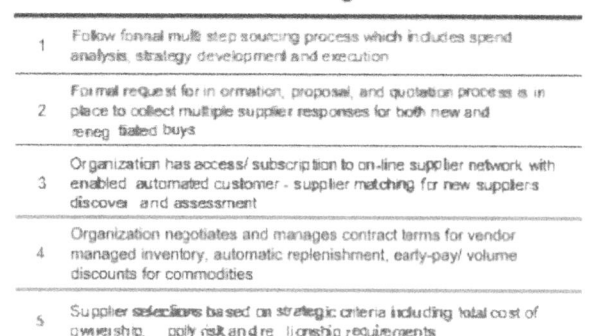

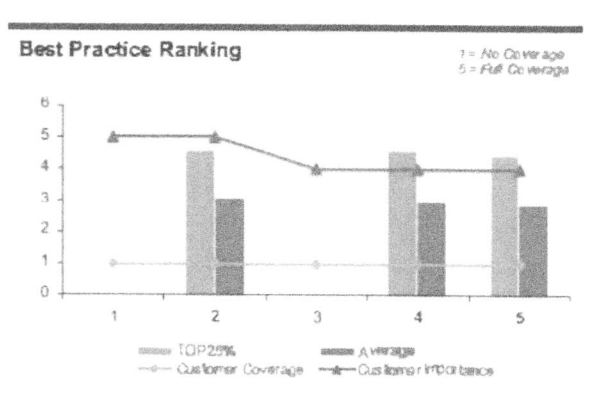

Please choose the correct answer.

a. Contract compliance is enforced through auto population of contract pricing on a purchase request
b. Invoices are automatically coded based on department, commodity or other business rules
c. System provides various standard analysis and reports to monitor purchasing operations and provide a detailed analysis of compliance related purchasing activities and procurement processes
d. Contract compliance against complex contract pricing structures, such as tiered or volume—based pricing, is automatically used to validate pricing on requisitions, POs and invoices

Answer: c

Explanation:

System provides various standard analysis and reports to monitor purchasing operations and provide a detailed analysis of compliance related purchasing activities and procurement processes is the best practice for Compliance based on Purchase Orders

132. **For Contract Management, which of the following is the best practice adoption based on Maverick Spending?**

Please choose the correct answer.

a. Electronic repository with the ability to share contracts with other employees for collaboration, version control, searching and options to set reminders of key expiration/renewal dates
b. Organization has ability to monitor supplier compliance with contract terms; and performs regular reviews of contracts to insure terms and conditions are being met
c. Contract management system is integrated with e-RFX/ e-Auction system to pre-populate relevant information into the contract
d. None of the above

Answer: b

Explanation:

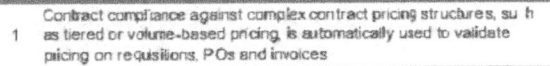

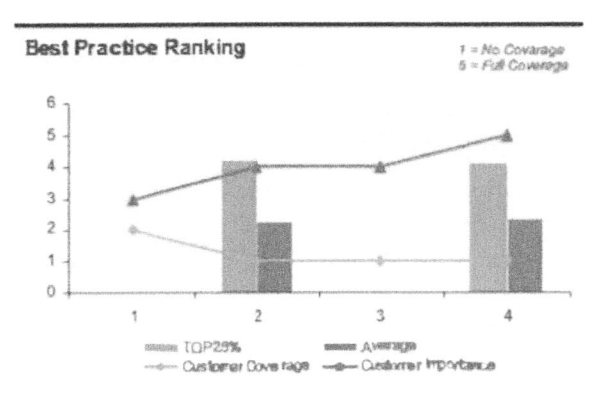

Organization has ability to monitor supplier compliance with contract terms; and performs regular reviews of contracts to insure terms and conditions are being met is the best practice for Contract Management based on Maverick Spending

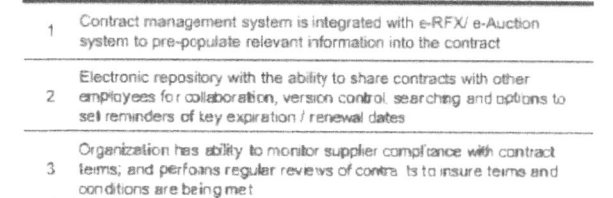

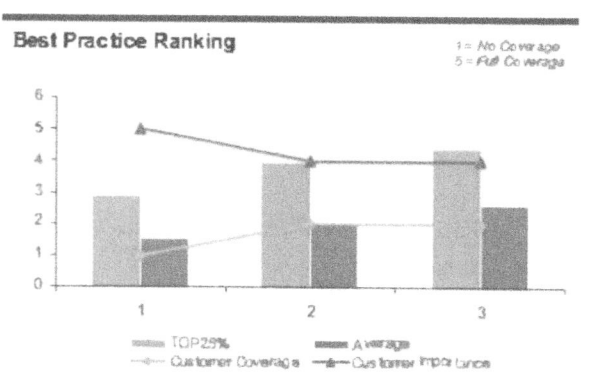

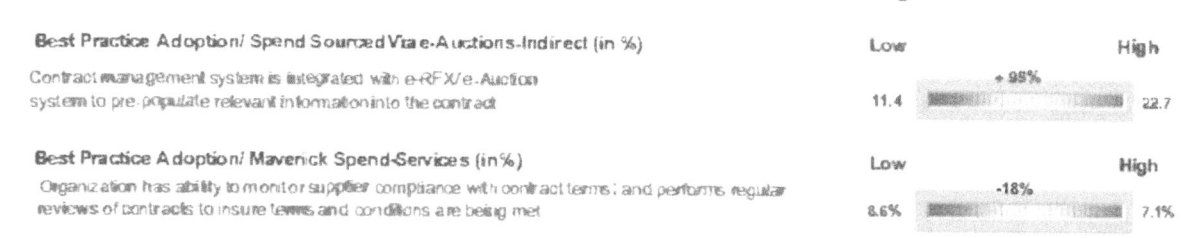

133. **For Requisitioning, which of the following is the best practice adoption based on Procurement FTEs?**

Please choose the correct answer.

a. Online item catalogs are used for self-services requisition
b. The ability to view ad approve purchase requests is available via email and mobile devices
c. System enables online order approvals as well as workflow and employs an electronic approval process for shopping carts and purchase requisitions
d. Approval levels are established based on risk; High risk/dollar requests require more stringent approvals, low risk/dollar requests require less stringent approvals

Answer: a

Explanation:

Online item catalogs are used for self-services requisition is the best practice for Requisitioning based on Procurement FTEs.

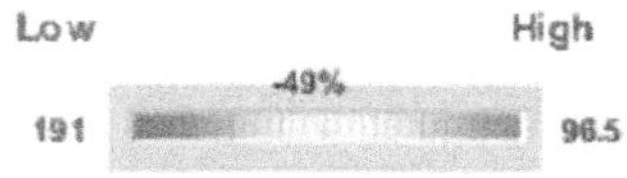

134. **For Order Processing, which of the following is the best practice adoption based on PO Error Rate?**

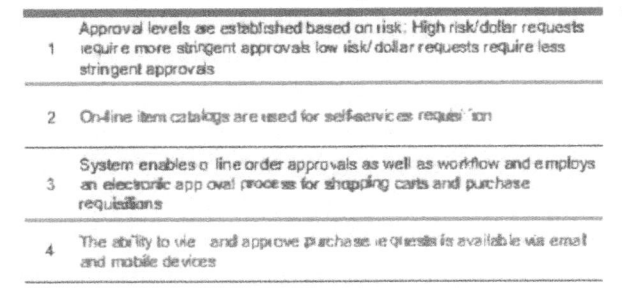

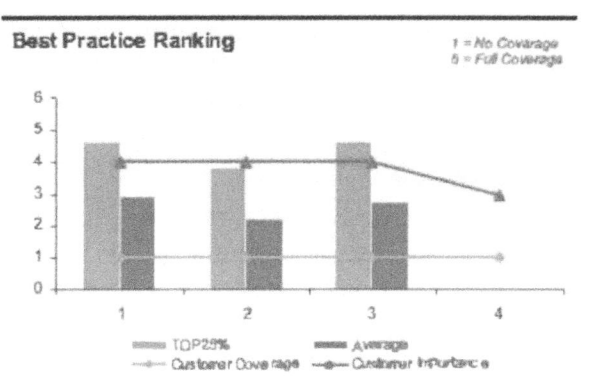

Please choose the correct answer.

a. Blanket purchase orders are used by the purchasing system for non-inventory items to reduce manual transactions and help forecasting
b. Buyers have online access to PO status
c. System processes PO automatically (no intervention necessary) and submits them electronically to suppliers
d. None of the above

Answer: c

Explanation:

System processes PO automatically (no intervention necessary) and submits them electronically to suppliers is the best practice for Order Processing based on PO Error Rate.

Best Practice Listing

1	Blanket purchase orders are used by the purchasing system for non-inventory items to reduce manual transactions and help forecasting
2	Buyers have online access to PO status
3	Change orders/PO acknowledgements are confirmed and re-communicated to the supplier electronically
4	System processes POs automatically (no intervention necessary) and submits them electronically to suppliers

Best Practice Ranking
1 = No Coverage
5 = Full Coverage

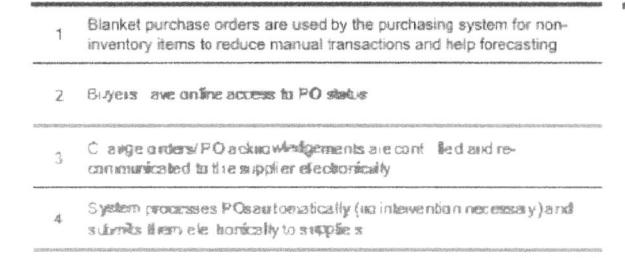

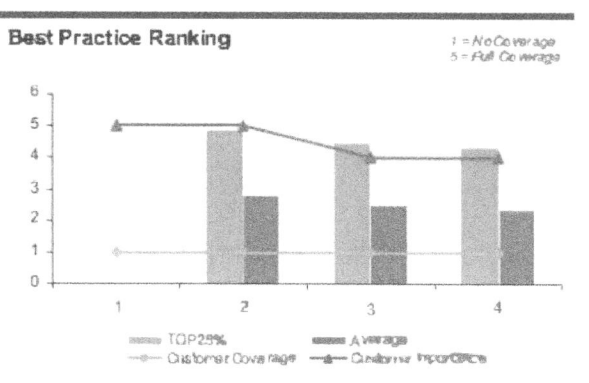

TOP 25% — Average — Customer Coverage — Customer Importance

Best Practices for Order Processing: Impact on PO Error Rate and POs Requiring Expediting

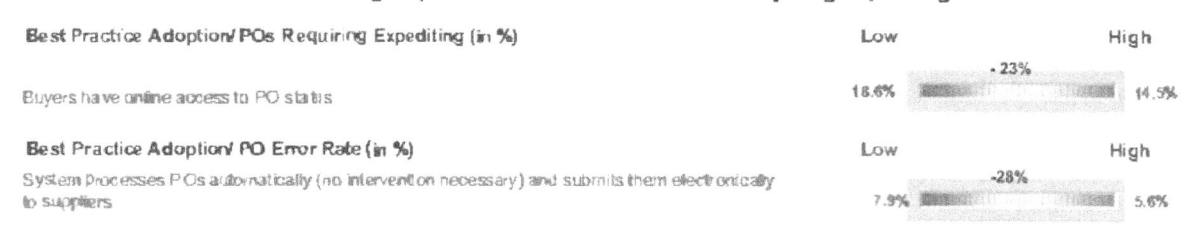

Best Practice Adoption/ POs Requiring Expediting (in %) — Low — High
Buyers have online access to PO status — 18.6% — -23% — 14.5%

Best Practice Adoption/ PO Error Rate (in %) — Low — High
System Processes POs automatically (no intervention necessary) and submits them electronically to suppliers — 7.9% — -28% — 5.6%

135. **For Material Receipt, which of the following is the best practice adoption based on Procurement Cost?**

    Please choose the correct answer.

    a. Evaluated receipt settlement is utilized to take advantage of early payment discount
    b. Receiving system is highly integrated with other systems such as purchasing and inventory systems
    c. Buyers have online access to PO status
    d. None of the above

    Answer: a

    Explanation:

    Evaluated receipt settlement is utilized to take advantage of early payment discount is the best practice for Material Receipt based on Procurement Cost.

Best Practice Listing

1	Evaluated receipt settlement is utilized to take advantage of early payment discount
2	Receiving system is highly integrated with other systems such as purchasing and inventory systems

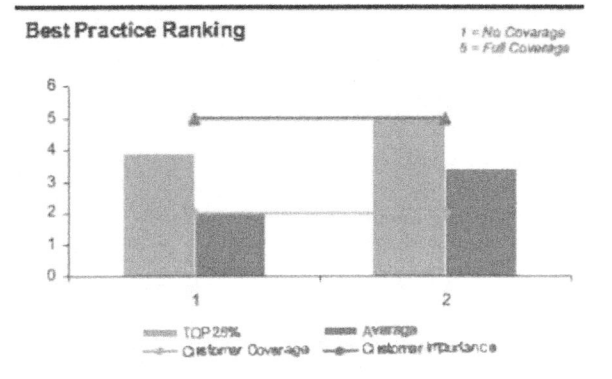

Best Practice Ranking

Best Practices for Material Receipt: Impact on Procurement Cost

Best Practice Adoption/ Procurement Cost (% of Total Spend)

Evaluated receipt settlement is utilized to take advantage of early payment discount — 2.6% to 0.9% (-54%)

136. **For Financial Settlement, which of the following is the best practice adoption based on Procurement Cost?**

Please choose the correct answer.

a. Company has supplier discount terms policy and compliance program to optimize capital through extension of days payable outstanding and discounts earned
b. AP managers spend time monitoring and evaluating AP processes rather than entering invoices into the system
c. Suppliers have visibility into payment status including invoice status, expected payment date and expected discount amount
d. The AP system automatically alerts and does not accept receipt of goods when it finds differences between invoice, order and receipt (within defined tolerances)

Answer: b

Explanation:

AP managers spend time monitoring and evaluating AP processes rather than entering invoices into the system is the best practice for Financial Settlement based on Procurement Cost.

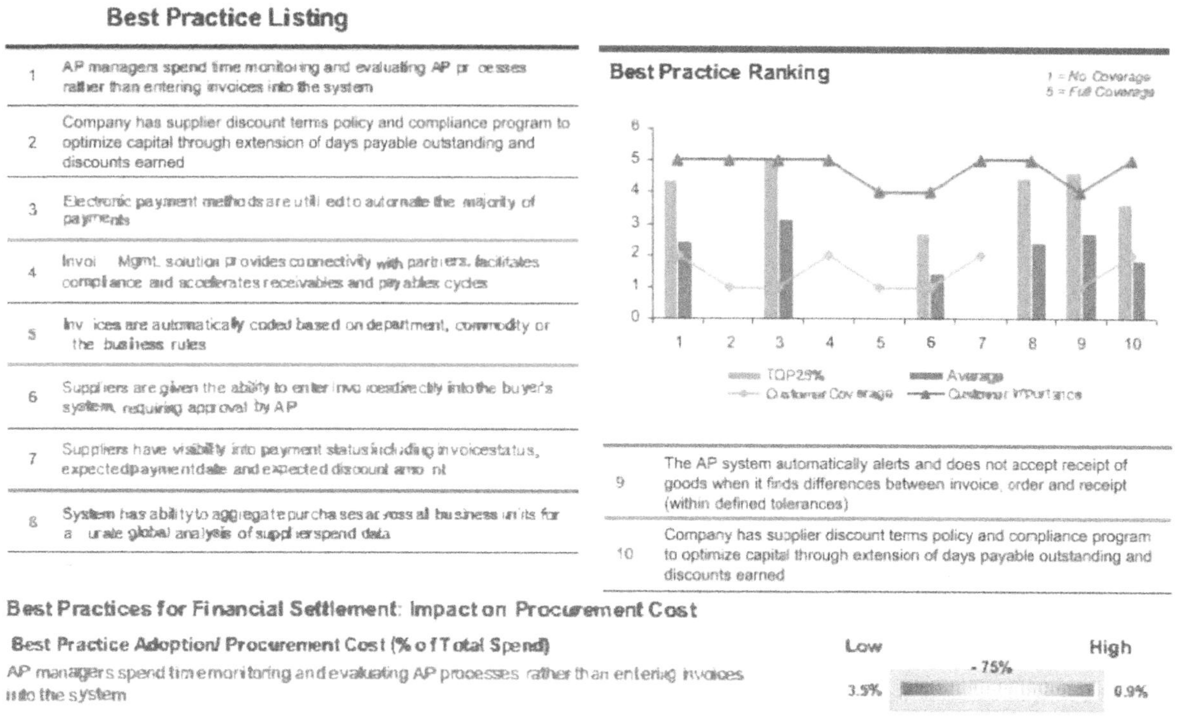

Procurement Knowledge

137. **Which of the following are benefits from Ariba Discovery?**

    Note: There are 3 correct answers to this question.

    a. Effective
    b. Integrated
    c. Trusted
    d. Mitigates Supply Risk
    e. Reduces attrition rate

    Answer: a, b, c

    Explanation:

    Ariba Discovery is the premier service for matching business buyers and sellers globally:

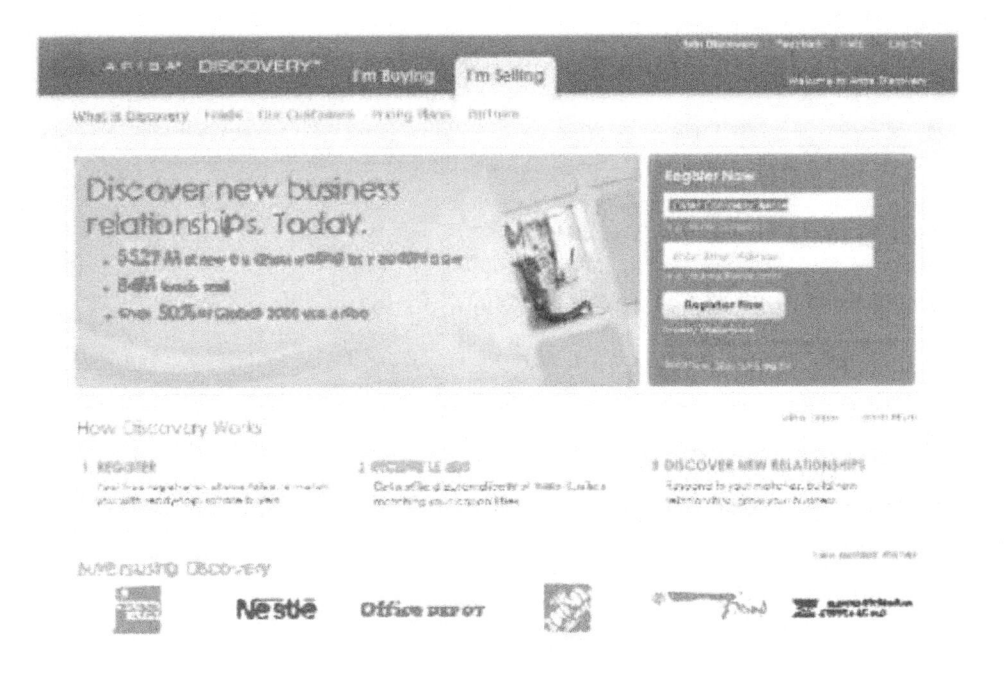

- Easy access to an active community of 3,000 leading buying organizations
- Matching service that proactively delivers relevant opportunities directly to your fingertips
- Rich profile building functionalities to differentiate your products and services to targeted buyers
- Advanced collaboration capabilities to network with your prospects

Benefits from Ariba Discovery:

- It's free!
- Fast & Easy. Save up to 90% time and 75% cost
- Effective
- Trusted
- Interactive
- Integrated

138. **Ariba Discovery sends email notifications to suppliers when you do which of the following?**

    Note: There are 3 correct answers to this question.

    a. Indicate you are not interested in a supplier's response
    b. Save a supplier
    c. Respond to a supplier's question
    d. Reopen a posting

e. Remove a supplier

Answer: a, b, c

Explanation:

Ariba Discovery Notifications:

Ariba Discovery sends email notifications to suppliers when you do the following:

- Award a supplier
- Indicate you are not interested in a supplier's response
- Save a supplier
- Close a posting
- Respond to a supplier's question

Ariba Discovery sends email notifications to purchasing agents:

- When suppliers send questions and
- When suppliers submit responses to postings

Setting Visibility and Notification Options:

Ariba Discovery's visibility and notification settings let you:

- Choose whether your company profile is visible to suppliers on postings you create.
- Choose whether you receive email notifications for certain actions and events.
- Create a company alias to display when you want to hide your company name in a posting.

139. **Which of the following statements are true regarding Rating suppliers?**

    Note: There are 2 correct answers to this question.

    a. You can only rate suppliers that you have interacted with.
    b. You can only rate a supplier once per posting.
    c. Ratings are temporary
    d. A supplier's average rating doesn't appear publicly on Ariba Discovery

    Answer: a, b

    Explanation:

    Setting Visibility and Notification Options:

    Ariba Discovery's visibility and notification settings let you:

- Choose whether your company profile is visible to suppliers on postings you create.
- Choose whether you receive email notifications for certain actions and events.
- Create a company alias to display when you want to hide your company name in a posting.

About supplier ratings:

- You can only rate suppliers that you have interacted with.
- You can only rate a supplier once per posting.
- Ratings are permanent.
- A supplier's average rating appears publicly on Ariba Discovery.

140. **Which of the following is/are way(s) to initiate a Supplier Discovery Posting?**

    Please choose the correct answer.

    a. During the Event Creation Process
    b. Creating Postings Directly in Ariba Discovery
    c. Both a and b
    d. None of the above

    Answer: c

    Explanation:

    About supplier ratings:

    - You can only rate suppliers that you have interacted with.
    - You can only rate a supplier once per posting.
    - Ratings are permanent.
    - A supplier's average rating appears publicly on Ariba Discovery.

    Creating Supplier Discovery Postings:

    There are several ways to initiate a Supplier Discovery Posting:

    - During the Event Creation Process
    - Creating Postings Directly in Ariba Discovery

141. **In Ariba sourcing, how many types of sourcing events exist?**

    Please choose the correct answer.

    a. 2
    b. 3
    c. 4

d. 5

Answer: c

Explanation:

What is the Ariba Sourcing™ solution?

- An application developed for you to conduct sourcing events online.
- An application that empowers you with:
    - Online sourcing functionality
    - Competitive bidding
    - Advanced bid analysis tools
    - Multi-language, multi-currency features

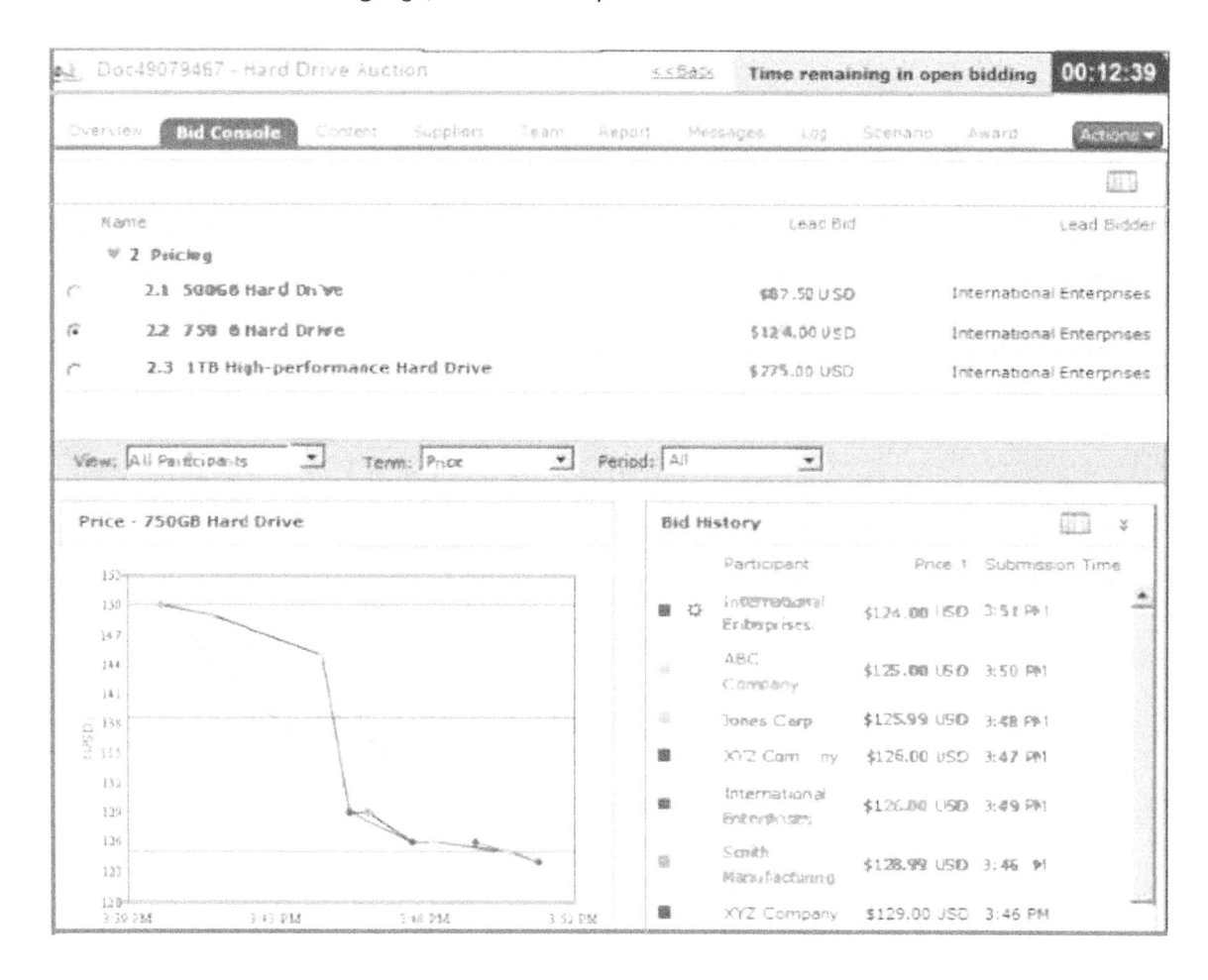

Event Types:

There are 4 types of sourcing events:

- Request for Information (RFI)
- Request for Proposal (RFP)
- 2 Auctions

142. **Which of the following are Forward Auction types?**

    Note: There are 2 correct answers to this question.

    a. Forward Auction with Bid Transformation
    b. Total Cost Auction
    c. Dutch Forward Auction
    d. Dutch Forward Auction with Bid Transformation

    Answer: a, c

    Explanation:

    Auction Overview:

    - Dynamic online bidding session where bidders submit legally binding bids.
    - Transfers the negotiation process from project owners and their bidders to bidders and their competitors.
    - Project Owners can evaluate bids and make award decisions online.
    - Price is the most important factor.

Reverse Auctions:

- Auctions for buying are Reverse Auctions.
  - HERE: Bids decrease over time.
- Reverse Auctions types:
  - Reverse Auction with Bid Transformation
  - Total Cost Auction
  - Dutch Reverse Auction
  - Dutch Reverse Auction with Bid Transformation

Forward Auctions:

- Auctions for selling are Forward Auctions.
  - HERE: Bids increase over time.
- Forward Auction types:
  - Forward Auction with Bid Transformation
  - Dutch Forward Auction

143. **Which of the following are benefits from Request for Proposal (RFP)?**

    Please choose the correct answer.

a. Good for sourcing of standard items
b. Allows for exploration and comparison of a variety of possible options
c. Enables suppliers to differentiate themselves
d. Only b and c
e. All of the above

Answer: d

Explanation:

Request for Proposal (RFP):

An event used to solicit proposals from potential suppliers. Price is not the only factor.

Closed RFPs:

- Gather competitive market information without revealing feedback to suppliers
- Can be used as qualifying round to narrow the supply base

Competitive RFPs:

- Suppliers see competitive information (rank and/or price) in real time and submit multiple bids to out-bid their competitors
- Differs from an auction since the focus is not just on collecting final pricing

Benefits from RFP:

- Good for sourcing of non-standard items
- Allows for exploration and comparison of a variety of possible options
- Enables suppliers to differentiate themselves

144. Which of the following is/are example(s) of Approvables?

    Please choose the correct answer.

    a. Contract Requests
    b. Invoice Reconciliations
    c. Supplier Data Updates
    d. Only b, c
    e. All of the above

    Answer: e

    Explanation:

    An approvable is a document that must be approved by designated users before it can be acted upon.

A requester prepares and submits an approvable document and the Ariba Procurement Solution routes it to the designated approvers (for example, the supervisor of the requester). After the request is approved by the approvers, it can be acted upon. For example, after a purchase requisition is fully approved, the Ariba Procurement Solution generates a purchase order and sends it to the supplier.

- An approvable is a document that must be affirmed by a designated approver before it can be acted upon.
- Examples include:
    - Requisitions
    - Contract Requests User Profile Changes
    - Supplier Data Updates (Catalog Updates)
    - Receipts
    - Invoice Reconciliations

145. **How many types of approvers can be present on an approval graph?**

    Please choose the correct answer.

    a. 2
    b. 3
    c. 4
    d. 5

    Answer: a

    Explanation:

    Approver Types:

    There are two types of approvers who can be on an approval graph:

    Required Approvers - A user or a group who is required to approve a document before it can progress. Required approvers might be managers of the requestor, department or cost center, or people in your A/P or Finance group. They receive immediate notification by email that their approval is required. When an approver logs into the Ariba Procurement Solution, all approvables that require action are listed in the To Do area on their home page. The approver can open the approvable document to examine it and can either approve or deny it. (With a few exceptions - for example, Invoice Reconciliation documents cannot be denied. They can be either approved or rejected, which sends them back to the supplier so that the supplier generates a new invoice.)

    Watchers - A user or group who is notified of the submission and status of an approvable, but who cannot approve or deny the document. There are many circumstances when individuals might need to monitor a request through the approval process, though they do not have the authority or there is no business need for them to approve or deny it. For example, a user could be added as a watcher on a requisition if the requisition is created by another user on their behalf. Or, facilities personnel might like to know whenever office furniture is purchased, so they can make logistical arrangements to receive and deliver the furniture to the requester.

Approver Types

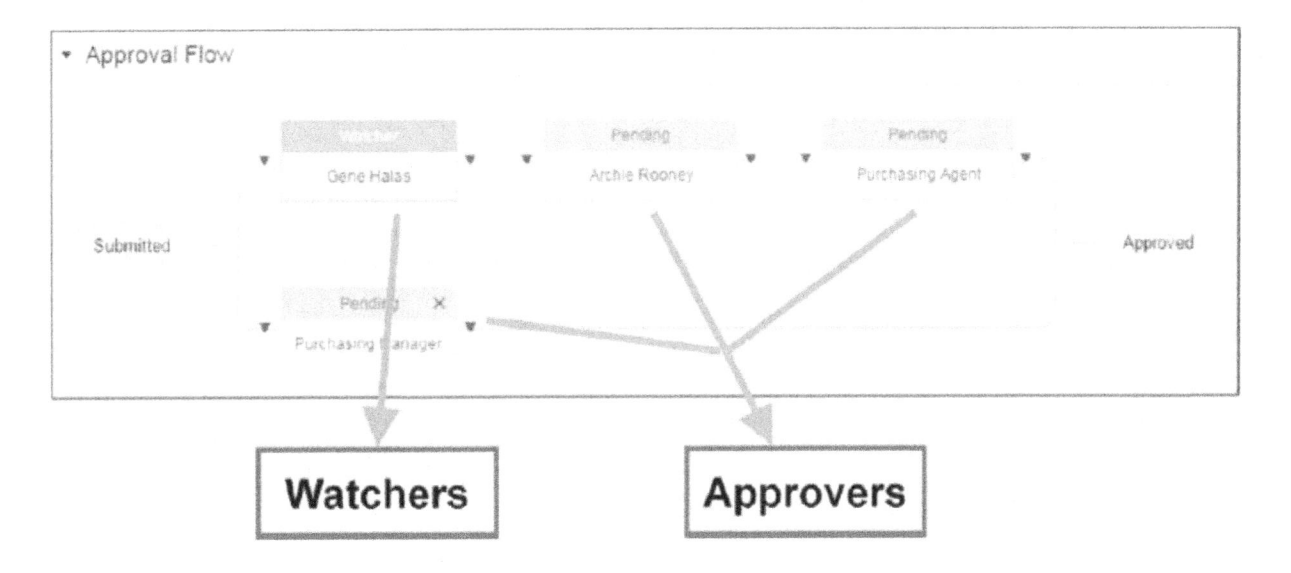

146. **If there are multiple approvers, those approvers can be arranged in which of the following?**

    Please choose the correct answer.

    a. Parallel
    b. Serial
    c. Either a or b
    d. None of the above

    Answer: c

    Explanation:

    Types of Routing:

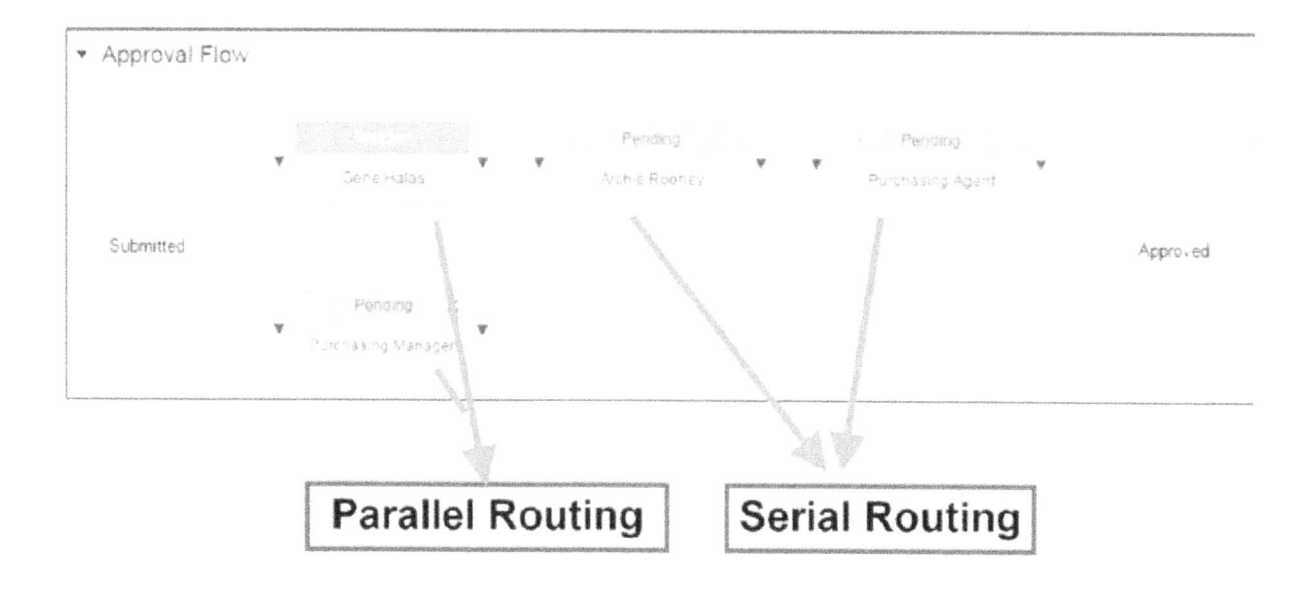

Approval Flow

[Approval flow diagram showing Submitted → Gene Halas (Pending) → Archie Rooney (Pending) → Purchasing Agent (Pending) → Approved, with parallel branch through Purchasing Manager (Pending). Labels indicate "Parallel Routing" and "Serial Routing".]

The Approval Flow screen shows the approval graph for a particular approvable. The approval graph displays the approvers to whom the document will be routed and the order in which the routing will occur. They are automatically generated through the approval rules that your administrator configures.

If there are multiple approvers, those approvers can be arranged in either:
- **Parallel:** All approvers in parallel are simultaneously notified about the document needing approval. In the approval graph above, Gene Halas and the Purchasing Manager group are parallel approvers. The document is routed to both of them at the same time.
- **Serial:** Certain approvers are notified only after earlier approvers have approved the document. In the approval graph above, Archey Rooney and Purchasing Agent are serial in the flow, after Gene Halas.

ALL the required approvers on an approval graph must approve the document in order for that document to be considered fully approved and move further through the system. Approvable documents are approved or denied **in their entirety,** not piecemeal. For example, a requisition, even if it contains multiple line items, is either entirely approved or entirely denied. The individual line items on that requisition cannot be approved or denied individually.

147. **An approval node can be which of the following types?**

    Note: There are 3 correct answers to this question.

    a. Individual User
    b. Group
    c. Approval List
    d. Cluster
    e. Segment

    Answer: a, b, c

Explanation:

Types of Approval Nodes:

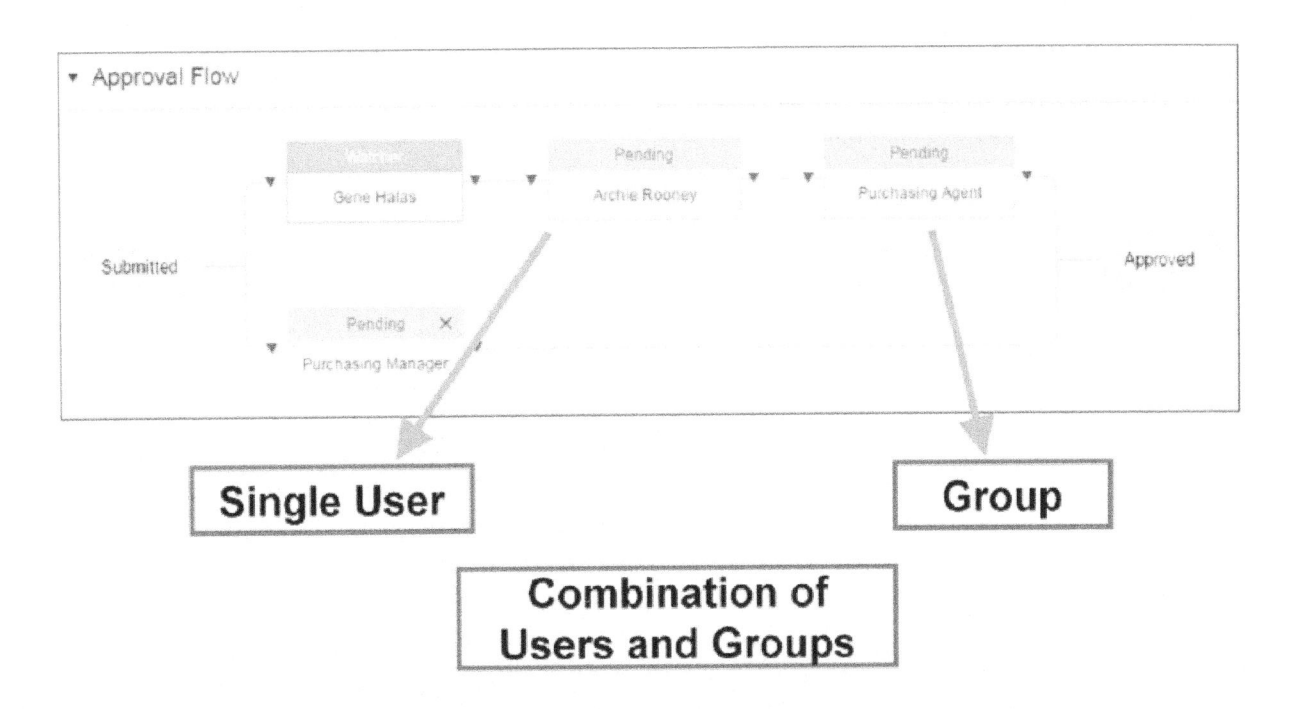

An approval node can be one of the following types:
- **Individual User** - The simplest approver is a user. A user is usually added to an approval flow because they are part of a supervisory chain or because they are somehow identified on the document being approved or a document related to the one being approved.
- **Group** - If an approval node is a group, any of the users who are members of that group can approve or deny the document. The first user to approve or deny the approvable completes the approval requirement and the request moves to the next node in the approval flow (or in the case of denial, the approvable is withdrawn). Groups must be predefined in the system and have users assigned as members in order to be used in approval logic.
- **Approval List** - An approval node can also be a list comprised of a combination of individual users and groups. The approval action of an approval list is similar to that of a group, in that the first user - whether they be an individual user named in the node or a member of a group named in the node - completes the approval requirement for the entire node.

Types of Approval Nodes

148. Approvers can receive an email notification under which of the following case(s)?

    Please choose the correct answer.

a. Someone submits or resubmits a document for approval
b. Someone withdraws a document
c. The system is about to escalate a request to a supervisor
d. Only b and c
e. All of the above

Answer: e

Explanation:

The Ariba Procurement Solution sends an email notification message to a user when that person becomes an active approver for a document.

Approvers can receive an email notification when:
- Someone submits or resubmits a document for approval
- Someone withdraws a document
- The system escalates a document
- The system is about to escalate a request to a supervisor

Multiple users receive the same email notification if they share a group responsibility. The ability to approve or deny is the same as in the Ariba Procurement Solution—the first one to approve or deny by replying to the email makes the decision.

Your organization might allow approvers to forward email approval notifications. Forwarding an approval notification delegates the approval authority to all recipients of the message. When an email approval notification message is forwarded, the approval graph continues to show the original approver, not the delegated approver. The ability to delegate through email forwarding is configurable by your administrator.

Email Approval Example

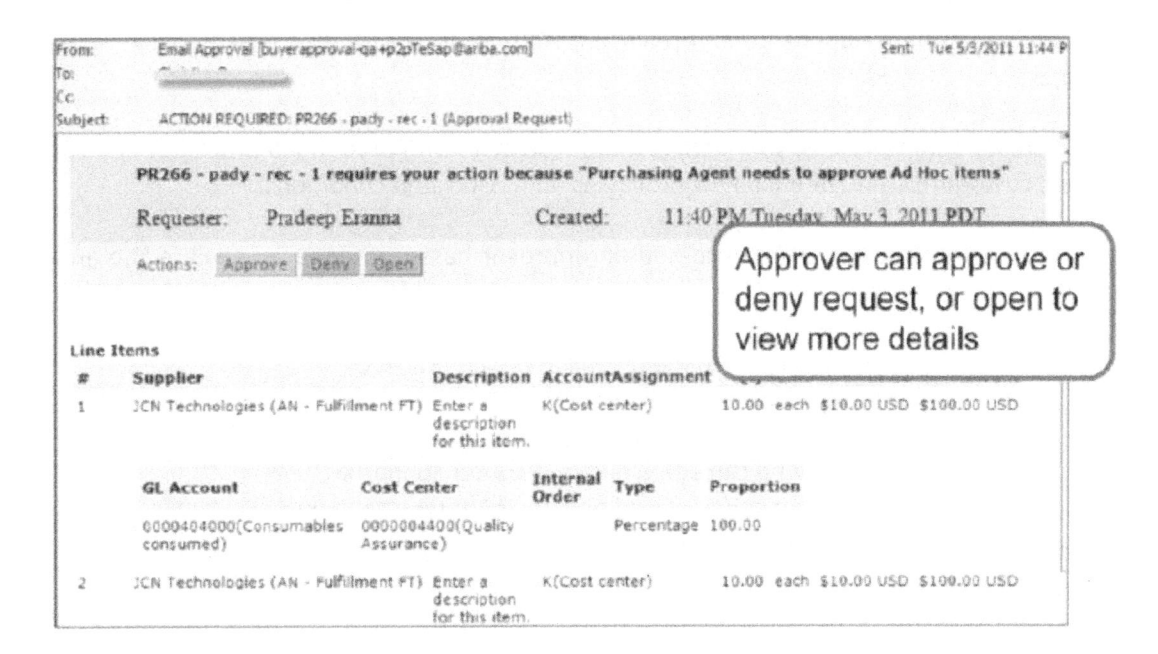

149. **Which of the following statements are true regarding Approval rules?**

    Note: There are 3 correct answers to this question.

    a. Your organization can only use default processes
    b. Approval rules determine the overall approval process
    c. Approval Processes interface manages versioning and audit-tracking
    d. There are unique rule sets based on document type and content
    e. The approval process formally starts after a document is created

    Answer: b, c, d

    Explanation:

    Approval Rules Basics:

    The approval process is a set of configurable approval rules that specify and define conditions and actions for a specific type of approvable. Approval rules determine who approves a document, the order of the approval requests, and who can edit a document after submittal. For example, for a requisition, you could have a rule stating that if the requester and the preparer are not the same, the requester must approve. The approval process formally starts after a document is submitted and is graphically depicted in the approval flow diagram.

The business logic of the approval rules depends on the type and the content of the approvable document such as requisitions, invoices, or contract requests. For example, you could have a rule that specifies that the AP Director must be included as an approver for every invoice greater than $100,000. Or, you could define a rule that forces Purchasing Agents to collaborate with a minimum of three suppliers and receive bids from all of them with a price below a set maximum price.

To create approval rules, your administrator can start with predefined processes and conditions and customize them, or build new processes and associated conditions.

The system can be configured to add an approver based on any user field in the approvable document.

- Approval rules determine the overall approval process:
    - Specify who approves a document
    - Set the order of approval requests
    - Control who can edit a document after submittal
- There are unique rule sets based on document type and content
- Your organization can use default or customized processes
- Approval Processes interface manages versioning and audit-tracking

150. **Which of the following statements are true regarding Rule-Builder Editor and Interpreter?**

    Note: There are 3 correct answers to this question.

    a. The rule interpreter is not real-time
    b. The rule-builder editor allows you to create and edit approval rules
    c. The rule interpreter reads and executes the approval rules
    d. The rule interpreter automatically generates the approval graphs
    e. The rule-builder editor automatically generates the approval graphs

    Answer: b, c, d

    Explanation:

    Approval Rules Engine:

    The Ariba Procurement Solution has a general-purpose approval engine that can be applied to any type of approvable document. This approval engine determines the approval process and is responsible for three main functions:
    1. Create the approval graph for each approvable document.
    2. Update the approval graph as different users approve, deny, or change the approvable.
    3. Route approval notifications to all involved users.

    Rule-Builder Editor and Interpreter - The approval engine includes a rule-builder editor and a rule interpreter. The rule-builder editor allows you to create and edit approval rules. The rule interpreter reads and executes the approval rules and automatically generates the approval graphs. The interpreter is real-time; any changes are immediately shown in the approval chart.

Error Messages - Before submission, a requisition can contain data that is inconsistent or otherwise contains errors. For example, a user can delete a required data value such as the cost center to which a line item is billed. However, the system will not allow the user to submit the approvable until all errors have been corrected. If an approvable contains errors, the Approval Flow screen will display those errors instead of the approval graph to help you find and correct the problems.

Made in the USA
Columbia, SC
23 July 2019